THE WORKBOOK ON
THE BEATITUDES

The Workbook on the Beatitudes

✠

Maxie Dunnam
and
Kimberly Dunnam Reisman

UPPER ROOM BOOKS®
NASHVILLE

Library of Congress Cataloging-in-Publication Data

Dunnam, Maxie D.
The workbook on the Beatitudes / Maxie Dunnam and Kimberly Dunnam Reisman.
    p. cm.
13-digit ISBN 978-0-8358-9808-9
10-digit ISBN 0-8358-9808-3
1. Beatitudes—Study and teaching. 2. Church group work. 3. Small groups. I. Reisman, Kimberly Dunnam, 1960–   II. Title.
BT382.D87 2005
241.5'3'071—dc22

2004018767

To the people of Trinity United Methodist Church, who have blessed me with their encouragement and support, and to the people of New Road, Trinity's "unconventional, modern approach to worship," who have blessed me with their perseverance, their willingness to walk with me in faith, and their openness to my preaching, guidance, and friendship.

—Kim Reisman

CONTENTS

INTRODUCTION

We usually associate mountains with far-reaching vistas, unobstructed views that stretch to a far horizon. The Beatitudes come from the mountain slopes above Capernaum, where, according to scripture and tradition, our Lord delivered the Sermon on the Mount. The Beatitudes form the core of that sermon.

Countless books have been written about the Beatitudes, seeking to explore the depths of this sublime teaching of Jesus. None of these books has ever exhausted the wealth of meaning in this passage. Certainly we have no thought of being able to do so. We simply seek to make available to the reader some of the profound lessons present in the Beatitudes.

When we wrote our previous workbook on the Ten Commandments, we intended to add a workbook on the Beatitudes. The Ten Commandments, from Mount Sinai, and the Beatitudes, from the mount in Capernaum, combine to provide for disciples of Jesus a way to be, to walk, and to relate. They also offer values and principles to guide our decisions.

Obvious contrasts exist between those words that came to Moses on Mount Sinai and these that came from Jesus. Moses was a servant of God; Jesus was the Son of God. When Moses spoke, the mountains quivered and God's words resounded like thunder; they were emblazoned on tablets of stone. Jesus' words were gentle and tender, written on fleshly tablets, so full of grace that they lodged in the human heart.

The Ten Commandments bear the notion of stormy and terrible judgment, while each Beatitude begins with *blessed* and reaches down to the humblest, the weakest, the weariest. The Ten Commandments state with bold clarity what we *must do and not do*. The Beatitudes come from the other direction: what we must *be* and *do* as members of Christ's family. Thus, the Sermon on the Mount, the core of which is the Beatitudes, is not so much a code of conduct as an invitation to kingdom living.

The Beatitudes contain more promise than demand. New Testament scholar Amos Wilder said that they have less to do with an ethic of obedience than with an ethic of grace. Yet it is still true that while the Beatitudes, in contrast to the Ten Commandments, are marked primarily by an inwardness rather than external expression, the "truth in the inward being" has markedly outward expression. This workbook is based on that conviction.

It is doubtful that anyone truly knows Christ unless that person follows Jesus daily. This is the message of the larger Sermon on the Mount, and certainly it is the message of the Beatitudes. In the four Gospels we learn and come to understand the man Jesus. We see him in his words and deeds and thereby discover his lifestyle. In the larger Sermon on the Mount, we are confronted with "the Jesus way" of life, which is concretely focused in the Beatitudes.

Being a disciple of Jesus is no light matter. Discipleship is a demanding way of life because a disciple is one who is disciplined to the attitudes and purposes of Christ.

Disciples identify themselves with a person and a body of teaching. Christian disciples are persons who, meeting God in Jesus Christ, continue to learn from Jesus. The test of our commitment as Christians is how we work out the meaning of that commitment in our lives after we enter into a relationship with Jesus.

The Beatitudes lay down principles of behavior for citizens of the kingdom. They contain a message about the lifestyle of the new creation—those who have been made new by Jesus Christ and are self-conscious residents of the kingdom. John Wesley expressed it this way:

> This is the religion we long to see established in the world, a religion of love and joy and peace, having its seat in the heart, in the inmost soul, but ever showing itself by its fruits, continually springing forth not only in all innocence . . . but likewise in every kind of beneficence, in spreading virtue and happiness all around it. (Wesley, "An Earnest Appeal to Men of Reason and Religion," *The Works of John Wesley*, 11:46)

How to Use This Workbook

This workbook, designed for individual and group use, calls for an eight-week commitment. We ask you to give about thirty minutes each day to reflecting on some aspect of the Beatitudes. For some persons, the thirty minutes will come at the beginning of the day. However, if you cannot give the time at the beginning of the day, do it whenever the time is available—but do it regularly. This workbook study is not only an intellectual pursuit but also a spiritual journey, the purpose of which is to assimilate the content into your daily life. This journey is personal, but we hope that you will share your insights with some fellow pilgrims who meet together once a week during the eight weeks of the study.

The workbook is arranged in eight major divisions, each designed to guide you for one week. Each week has seven daily readings containing three sections: (1) reading, (2) reflecting and recording thoughts about the material and your own understanding and experience, and (3) practical suggestions for weaving ideas from the reading into your daily life.

Quotations other than scripture are identified in parentheses at the end of each selection. The citation gives the author along with the book title and page number, website, or other source where the quotation may be found. These citations are keyed to the Sources section at the end of the workbook, where you will find complete bibliographic information should you wish to read certain works more fully.

Throughout the workbook you will see this symbol:

■ ■ ■

When you come to that symbol, please stop. Do not read further. Reflect as requested so that you will internalize the ideas shared or the experience reflected upon.

In our writing, each of us tells personal stories. We do not bother to identify which one tells a particular story. We believe that this style makes reading flow more naturally. Our teaching here is a cooperative enterprise that we seek to make as personal as possible.

Reflecting and Recording

After the reading each day, you are asked to record some of your reflections. The degree of meaning you receive from this workbook depends largely on your faithfulness in practicing its method. You may be unable on a particular day to do precisely what is requested. If so, simply record that fact and note why you can't follow through. On some days there may be more suggestions than you can deal with in the time you have available. Do what is most meaningful for you, and do not feel guilty about the rest.

Finally, always remember that this pilgrimage is personal. What you write in your workbook is *your* private property. For this reason, we do not recommend sharing the workbook. The importance of what you write is not what it may mean to someone else but what it means to you. Writing, even if only brief notes or single-word reminders, helps you clarify your thoughts and feelings.

The significance of the reflecting and recording dimension will grow as you move along. Even beyond the eight weeks, you will find meaning in looking back to what you wrote on a particular day in response to a particular situation.

Sharing the Journey with Others

In the history of Christian spirituality, the spiritual director or guide has been a significant person. To varying degrees, most of us have had spiritual directors—individuals to whom we have turned for support and direction in our spiritual pilgrimage. In a sense this workbook can become a spiritual guide since you can use it as a private venture without participating in a group.

The value of this workbook will be enhanced, however, if you share the adventure with eight to twelve others. (Larger numbers tend to limit individual involvement.) In this way, you will profit from the growing insights of others, and they will profit from yours. The text includes a guide for group meetings at the end of each week.

If a group is working through this book, everyone should begin the workbook on the same day so that when your group meets, all of you will have dealt with the same material and will be at the same place in the text. Beginning the adventure with an initial get-acquainted group meeting is a good idea. This introduction provides a guide for the initial meeting.

Group sessions for this workbook are designed to last one and one-half hours (except for the initial meeting). Participants covenant to attend all sessions unless an emergency prevents attendance. There will be eight weekly sessions in addition to the get-acquainted meeting.

Group Leader's Tasks

One person may provide the leadership for the entire eight weeks, or leaders may be assigned from week to week. The leader's tasks include the following:

1. Read the directions and determine ahead of time how to handle the session. You may not be able to use all the suggestions for sharing and praying together. Select those you think will be most meaningful and for which you have adequate time.
2. Model a style of openness, honesty, and warmth. Do not ask anyone to share anything he or she feels uncomfortable sharing. Usually, as leader, be the first to share, especially in the case of personal experiences.
3. Moderate the discussion.
4. Encourage reluctant members to participate and try to prevent a few group members from dominating the conversation.
5. Keep the sharing centered in personal experience rather than on academic debate.
6. Honor the time schedule. If it appears necessary to go longer than one and one-half hours, get consensus for continuing another twenty or thirty minutes.
7. See that the entire group knows the meeting time and place, especially if meetings are held in different homes.
8. See that the necessary materials for meetings are available and that the meeting room is arranged ahead of time.

Holding weekly meetings in the homes of participants is a good idea. (Hosts or hostesses should make sure there are as few interruptions as possible from children, telephones, pets, and so forth.) If the meetings are held in a church, plan to meet in an informal setting. Encourage participants to dress casually.

If refreshments are planned, serve them after the formal meeting. This will allow persons who wish to stay longer for informal discussion to do so, while those who need to keep to the time schedule may leave, having had the full value of the meeting time.

Suggestions for Initial Get-Acquainted Meeting

The initial meeting has two purposes: getting acquainted and beginning the shared pilgrimage. Here are ideas for getting started:

1. Ask each person in the group to give his or her full name and the name by which each wishes to be called. Address all persons by first name or nickname. If name tags are needed, provide them.

2. Let each person in the group share one of his or her happiest, most exciting, or most meaningful experiences during the past three or four weeks.

3. Ask any who are willing to share their expectations of this workbook study. Why did they become a part of the group study? What does each one expect to gain from it? What are his or her reservations?

4. Review the introduction and ask if anyone has questions about directions and procedures. (**Leader,** read the introduction before the meeting.) If people have not received copies of the workbook, hand out the books now. Remember that everyone must have a workbook.

5. Day 1 in the workbook is the day after this initial meeting; the next meeting should be held on Day 7 of the first week. If the group must choose a weekly meeting time other than seven days from this initial session, adjust the reading assignment so that the weekly meetings occur on Day 7, and Day 1 is the day after a group meeting.

6. Nothing binds group members together more than praying for one another. Encourage each participant to write the names of all individuals in the group in his or her workbook and to pray for them by name daily during the eight weeks.

7. After announcing the time and place of the next meeting, close with a prayer, thanking God for each person in the group, for the opportunity for growth, and for the possibility of growing through spiritual disciplines.

God bless you as you continue this workbook journey.

Week One

✠

Blessed Are You

✠

DAY 1

Who Is a God Like You?   *Numbers 6:24-26*

But they and our ancestors acted presumptuously and stiffened their necks and did not obey your commandments; they refused to obey, and were not mindful of the wonders that you performed among them; but they stiffened their necks and determined to return to their slavery in Egypt. But you are a God ready to forgive, gracious and merciful, slow to anger and abounding in steadfast love, and you did not forsake them. Even when they had cast an image of a calf for themselves and said, "This is your God who brought you up out of Egypt," and had committed great blasphemies, you in your great mercies did not forsake them in the wilderness. (Neh. 9:16-19*a*)

The LORD works vindication and justice for all who are oppressed.
He made known his ways to Moses, his acts to the people of Israel.
The LORD is merciful and gracious,
    slow to anger and abounding in steadfast love.
He will not always accuse, nor will he keep his anger forever.
He does not deal with us according to our sins,
    nor repay us according to our iniquities.
For as the heavens are high above the earth,
    so great is his steadfast love toward those who fear him;
as far as the east is from the west,
    so far he removes our transgressions from us. (Ps. 103:6-12)

The prophets and the psalmists sought desperately to communicate the nature of God. They had to repeat it over and over: God is gracious and compassionate, forgiving, slow to anger and abounding in love, extravagant with mercy and blessing, healing and redeeming, providing justice and hope. The prophet Micah, overcome with awe, struggled to express the depth of his understanding and his desire to share God's reaching out to us:

Who is a God like you, pardoning iniquity
  and passing over the transgression
  of the remnant of your possession?
He does not retain his anger forever,
  because he delights in showing clemency.
He will again have compassion upon us;
  he will tread our iniquities under foot. (Mic. 7:18-19)

Max Lucado talks about the difficulty in titling his book on the Beatitudes. He said that getting the right title was almost as difficult as writing the entire book. He and the editors at Word Publishing went through dozens of titles, discarding one after the other. They spent hours searching for the appropriate phrase to describe the heart of the book.

> In my mind, the scales were tipped in favor of *The Applause of Heaven* when my editor, Carol, read part of the manuscript to some of the Word executives. She read a portion of the book that describes our final journey into the city of God. She read some thoughts I wrote about God's hunger to have his children home, about how he longs to welcome us and may even applaud when we enter the gates.
>
> After Carol read this section, she noticed one of the men was brushing away a tear. He explained his emotion by saying, "It's hard for me to imagine God applauding for me."
>
> Can you relate?
>
> I can. Certain things about God are easy to imagine. I can imagine him creating the world and suspending the stars. I can envision him as almighty, all-powerful, and in control. I can fathom a God who knows me, who made me, and I can even fathom a God who hears me. But a God who is in love with me? A God who is crazy for me? A God who cheers for me?
>
> But that is the message of the Bible. Our Father is relentlessly in pursuit of his children. He has called us home with his word, paved the way with his blood, and is longing for our arrival. (Lucado, *The Applause of Heaven*, xi–xii)

Jesus clarified the message of the prophets and the psalmists. He is God's gift of love to us. When we know that Jesus is God speaking to us—pronouncing blessings—we take notice.

Not just the Beatitudes but the entire Sermon on the Mount opens Jesus' mind and heart to us. As we noted in the introduction, this is Matthew's summary of Jesus' teaching for his disciples—the essence and core of Jesus' message. This little chunk of the sermon invites us to live. It pronounces blessing upon those who are finding the Jesus way.

Reflecting and Recording

Spend a few minutes pondering the possibility of God's applauding for you.

■ ■ ■

(Whenever you see this symbol, stop and follow the suggestion for reflection.)

Reflect on the last few months. Recall some deed or manner of relating to another person that God might have ~~applauded~~. *stated* welldone my daughter

■ ■ ■

The following phrases describe God. Put a check mark (✔) beside the ones you have most difficulty accepting:

☐   ready to forgive   ☐   gracious and merciful
☐   slow to anger   ☐   abounding in steadfast love
☐   full of compassion   ☐   removes our transgressions from us

Spend the rest of your time reflecting on why you have difficulty accepting these descriptions of God. *Do you struggle with any aspect of God's love, mercy*

■ ■ ■

During the Day

Psalm 103:8-14 is printed on page 213. Cut out the affirmation card and place it somewhere you will see it often during the day (such as on the refrigerator door, car dashboard, or bathroom mirror). Read it as often as you have opportunity.

As you go through the day, look for actions and attitudes you think God would applaud.

DAY 2

An Exclamation of What Is

Oh, the joys of those who do not follow the advice of the wicked,
   or stand around with sinners,
   or join in with scoffers.
But they delight in doing everything the LORD wants;
   day and night they think about his law.

They are like trees planted along the riverbank,
    bearing fruit each season without fail.
Their leaves never wither, and in all they do, they prosper. . . .
For the LORD watches over the path of the godly,
    but the path of the wicked leads to destruction. (Ps. 1:1-3, 6, NLT)

The first psalm begins, "Oh, the joys of those who do not follow the advice of the wicked," a statement of fact. Persons "who do not follow the advice of the wicked, or stand around with sinners, or join in with scoffers"—individuals who delight in doing everything the Lord wants, who meditate on his law day and night—those persons are blessed. Indeed, the Psalms announce the nature of blessedness repeatedly.

Blessed are all who take refuge in him. (Ps. 2:12, NIV)

Blessed is the nation whose God is the LORD. (Ps. 33:12, NIV)

Happy are those who consider the poor. (Ps. 41:1)

Blessed are those whose strength is in you. (Ps. 84:5, NIV)

Blessed are they who maintain justice. (Ps. 106:3, NIV)

Happy are those who fear the LORD. (Ps. 112:1)

Over and over, the Psalms say "blessed is" or "blessed are." So do the Beatitudes. Each one has precisely the same form, beginning "blessed are." Originally there was no verb in the Beatitudes. Scottish New Testament scholar William Barclay reminds us that the "are" in the English translations did not appear in the original Greek or Hebrew text. That word was added to bring out the meaning of each sentence.

> Jesus did not speak the beatitudes in Greek; he spoke them in Aramaic, which was the kind of Hebrew people spoke in his day. Aramaic and Hebrew have a very common kind of expression, which is in fact an exclamation and which means, "O the blessedness of . . ." That expression (*ashere* in the Hebrew) is common in the Old Testament. For instance, the first Psalm begins in the Hebrew: "O the blessedness of the [one] that walketh not in the counsel of the ungodly" (Psalm 1:1), that is the form in which Jesus first spoke the beatitudes. The beatitudes are not simple statements; they are exclamations: "O the blessedness of the poor in spirit!" (Barclay, *The Gospel of Matthew*, rev. ed., 1:83)

This means that the Beatitudes are not an explanation for what might be—or could be; they are exclamations about what is. In the Beatitudes, Jesus announces the privilege that is ours: to share joyfully with God the very blessedness that fills God's heart. And it is ours now, not in some future time. "Blessed are you" and "O the blessedness of . . ." are exclamations of what is.

We call them Beatitudes because the word *beatitude* simply means "blessing." Our word *blessing* comes from two sources: the Latin word *beatitudo*, which means "consummate bliss," and the Greek word *makarios*, which describes a joy whose secret lies within. Such joy is self-contained—independent of circumstance, chance, and change. Barclay helps us more clearly understand by reminding us that the English word *happiness* contains the root *hap*, which means "chance."

> Human happiness is something which is dependent on the chances and the changes of life, something which life may give and which life may also destroy. The Christian blessedness is completely untouchable and unassailable. (Barclay, *The Gospel of Matthew*, rev. ed., 1:89)

So, *blessed* means more than "happy"; it means joy of the highest kind. Jesus spoke of this joy as joy that no one will take away. (See John 16:22.)

Reflecting and Recording

Looking back over the past ~~few months of your life~~ year, think of experiences that made you happy. List four or five of those with a few words to describe them.

Now, think about the joy in your life. Have you known joy as Jesus would talk about it, even when you might not have been "happy"?

■ ■ ■

During the Day

Continue seeking to identify actions and attitudes God would applaud. Read the affirmation card for Psalm 103:8-14 several times throughout the day.

✠

DAY 3

Nonrational Paradox

When Jesus saw the crowds, he went up the mountain; and after he sat down, his disciples came to him. Then he began to speak, and taught them, saying: "Blessed are the poor in spirit, for theirs is the kingdom of heaven. Blessed are those who mourn, for they will be comforted. Blessed are the meek, for they will inherit the earth. Blessed are those who hunger and thirst for righteousness, for they will be filled. Blessed are the merciful, for they will receive mercy. Blessed are the pure in heart, for they will see God. Blessed are the peacemakers, for they will be called children of God. Blessed are those who are persecuted for righteousness' sake, for theirs is the kingdom of heaven." (Matt. 5:1-10)

We will not go so far as to say that the Beatitudes are irrational, but certainly they are nonrational—a nonrational paradox. How they differ from the way we normally think; how they directly counter those principles that seem to rule in human society.

I know a seminary student who is walking through some dark days. He and his wife have three children. He was an engineer, making a lot of money, living the so-called "American dream," settled into the pattern of seeking position, power, and success. Then God confronted him with a call to ministry. He wrestled with that call for two years before coming to seminary to prepare for ministry. Then his wife was diagnosed with cancer, the kind doctors offer little hope of curing. Thrust into a valley of near despair, this young man mourns; his heart is crushed. Who would call him blessed?

I think of a woman I met in Cuba. When Castro came to power, Cuba had thirty-eight Methodist missionaries; all had to leave. There were seventy Methodist pastors; all but two left. Methodist churches were closed—as were the churches of many other denominations. Little hope was given for the survival of the Christian faith. In the late 1980s, the bishop of the Methodist Church called for young people to make a commitment to be the leaven of the Christian faith in a land that now prided itself in being communist, totally materialistic and secular. Scores of Methodist young people responded. They studied the Bible, fasted and prayed, joined together in a community of mutual accountability and support. They were soon identified by the government as "cultural misfits." In the earlier days of the revolution, they probably would have been imprisoned. But the communist cause around the world was fading—in fact, dying—and overt punishment was not the pattern at that time in Cuba. Still, persecution existed. My friend was not admitted to a university. No reason was given, but she knew. Who would pronounce that persecution blessed?

The Beatitudes are a nonrational paradox. They run counter to the principles that rule human society and check the impulses that cause our ambitions to run wild.

Notice that each of these qualities of blessedness in the Beatitudes implies and suggests its opposite. Poverty implies the possibility of wealth; sorrow, the possibility of joy; humility, the possibility of pride; justice, the possibility of oppression; mercy, the possibility of indifference; peacemaking, the possibility of hostility; and persecution, the possibility of safety. So, in the Beatitudes, we see the hungers, hurts, and hopes that motivate the blessed ones. We get a vivid picture of the concerns that direct their lives, the passion that energizes their spirit.

In the pronouncement of what is blessed, we also get a picture of true joy. As we indicated yesterday, *blessed* means more than happy; it means the kind of joy that, according to Jesus, no one will take away. Sorrow and loss, pain and grief are powerless to touch this joy. It is a nonrational paradox—a joy that nothing in life or death can take away.

Reflecting and Recording

The following situations often affect our happiness. Make some notes about how these situations have shaped your happiness at one time or another.

ill health

loss of job or money

failure of a plan

broken relationship

failed friendship

geographic relocation

Can you identify a joy in your life even during these times when you were sad or disappointed?

During the Day

The Beatitudes are printed on page 213. Cut out the affirmation card and carry it with you during the day. Read the Beatitudes as often as possible, seeking to memorize them.

DAY 4

Repent, for the Kingdom Is at Hand

Now when Jesus heard that John had been arrested, he withdrew to Galilee. He left Nazareth and made his home in Capernaum by the sea, in the territory of Zebulun and Naphtali, so that what had been spoken through the prophet Isaiah might be fulfilled:
    "Land of Zebulun, land of Naphtali,
    on the road by the sea, across the Jordan,
        Galilee of the Gentiles—
    the people who sat in darkness have seen a great light,
    and for those who sat in the region and shadow of death
        light has dawned."
From that time Jesus began to proclaim,
"Repent, for the kingdom of heaven has come near." (Matt. 4:12-17)

As we have already indicated, the Beatitudes are set in the Sermon on the Mount. Notice where Matthew places that sermon in his Gospel narrative. The first event recorded in chapter 4 is the temptation of Jesus. After his baptism, before initiating his public ministry, Jesus went into the wilderness to fast and pray. This was a time of preparation, of testing and proving. Three times the devil tempted him, and three times Jesus resisted.

Satan: "Turn these stones into bread and prove your power" (AP).

Jesus: "We don't live by bread alone, but by every word that comes from the mouth of God" (AP).

Satan: "Throw yourself from the temple and prove God's care for you" (AP).

Jesus: "I will not put the Lord my God to the test. . . . I know that he will care for me—why test God?" (AP).

Satan: "Bow down and worship me, and I will give you the kingdoms of the world" (AP).

Jesus: "Get out of here, Satan; I will worship the Lord my God and will serve only God" (AP).

Having wrestled with Satan and completely rejected the way of power, materialism, and self-aggrandizement, abandoning himself to the Father with no strings attached, Jesus proved himself as God's Son and was ready to go public: "From that time on Jesus began to preach, 'Repent, for the kingdom of heaven is near'" (Matt. 4:17, NIV).

The initial call to everyone is to *repent*—a powerful word that means to change one's mind, in fact, to get a new mind. It means to be deeply sorry for past sins and to be willing to walk in a new manner and in a new direction. When Jesus called persons to repent, he was asking not only that they change their way of thinking and acting but also that they enter a totally new life. Forsaking the wrong way is one side of the coin of repentance; accepting the right way is the other side. So, in the same breath that Jesus calls us to repentance, he makes a glorious announcement: "The kingdom of heaven is at hand" (KJV).

Jesus proclaimed the kingdom of God as good news. The fact that the kingdom of God was at hand offered hope. Only when persons had accepted the kingdom could it be said that they had truly repented. To enter the kingdom was to be saved, to find eternal life. The Sermon on the Mount sums up what it means to be a kingdom person, to live in the kingdom. The Beatitudes are concrete expressions of the nature of kingdom life.

Before we explore each of these Beatitudes, which are laws or maxims of the kingdom—qualities of the blessedness of the kingdom of heaven expressed in earthly living—let's take a broad look at the nature of the kingdom. The foundation of the kingdom is "the revelation that God is Father, that Jesus Christ is his Son and the rightful Lord of the faithful, and that the Holy Spirit is the guide of all citizens of the kingdom. Believers, by identification with the Son, become sons [children] of the Father. The result is a . . . family, of those who so believe." (Jordan, *Sermon on the Mount*, 14).

Kingdom residents have a single loyalty: the kingdom takes precedence over everything else—occupation, family ties, possessions. To live in the kingdom means to put first things first, to seek the pearl of great price and to sacrifice everything in order to own that pearl. (See Matthew 13:45-46.) It demands a single loyalty.

Kingdom reality defines the life of kingdom residents. The kingdom, or "things of the kingdom" (Acts 19:8), does not refer to a portion of one's life but extends to every area. Jesus preached, addressing persons' spiritual needs; he taught, responding to their mental concerns and questions; he healed, attending to their physical wholeness.

Reflecting and Recording

To live in the kingdom means to have a single loyalty—to live as Christ would have you live. Spend some time examining your life in light of this claim. Do so particularly in relation to the following areas:

your occupation

■ ■ ■

your family

■ ■ ■

other relationships

■ ■ ■

material possessions

■ ■ ■

During the Day

Continue to read and memorize the Beatitudes.

DAY 5

Conversion and Reversal

Then Jesus went with them to a place called Gethsemane; and he said to his disciples, "Sit here while I go over there and pray." He took with him Peter and the two sons of Zebedee, and began to be grieved and agitated. Then he said to them, "I am deeply grieved, even to death; remain here and stay awake with me." And going a little farther, he threw himself on the ground and prayed, "My Father, if it is possible, let this cup pass from me; yet not what I want but what you want." (Matthew 26:36-39)

Not once but three times in Gethsemane, Jesus prayed, "My Father . . . may this cup be taken from me. Yet not as I will, but as you will" (v. 39, NLT).

He was agonizing over the inevitable cross. In a sense, this was one of his unanswered prayers. But not really, for this cry for deliverance was caught up in the ultimate commitment of his life: "Not what I will, but what you will."

Dietrich Bonhoeffer used this Gethsemane experience as the image and the act of becoming a Christian:

> When a man really gives up trying to make something out of himself . . . when in the fullness of tasks, questions, success or ill-hap, experiences and perplexities, a man throws himself into the arms of God . . . then he wakes with Christ in Gethsemane. That is faith . . . and it is thus he becomes a man and Christian. (G. Leibholz, quoting Bonhoeffer in "Memoir," in Dietrich Bonhoeffer, *The Cost of Discipleship*, 19)

We don't reflect enough on the radical change involved in becoming a Christian. It begins with faith—faith in Christ and Christ alone. Such faith calls us to repent of our past lifestyle, which has been totally self-centered, and to commit ourselves to a completely Christ-centered lifestyle. Christianity involves willingness to bear a cross. It calls for behavioral and relational change. We submit our lives to the power of God and yield ourselves to the life-giving influence of Jesus Christ. We become so yielded, so committed to the process of seeking and finding the kingdom, seeking and finding the living God in such a powerful way, that we desire God's authority above all.

This reality is not always obvious. Like the tiny mustard seed growing into a large plant (Matt. 13:31-32), or like the small lump of leaven put into the dough, permeating the whole loaf (13:33), we can't see, and certainly we cannot control, God's presence in our life. We submit to its hidden and powerful dynamic. So, even our desire to seek God's reign takes time. It demands attention, reflection, and an ongoing willingness to be what Jesus called us to be and do—and that's what the Beatitudes are all about.

Yesterday we noted that it is significant that the Beatitudes are set in the Sermon on the Mount. That sermon is a kingdom document. In the kingdom, God is the sovereign authority and demands total commitment. "No one can serve two masters," Jesus said in Matthew 6:24. God, who is sovereign, is our Father. We can completely yield ourselves to God, knowing that God's will for us is blessed.

The kingdom motif and the call to repentance and conversion pervade Matthew's Gospel. Indeed, in this Gospel Jesus consistently links announcement of the kingdom to the call for converting one's life. One must repent (4:17); one must sell everything to purchase the kingdom's pearl (13:45-46); one must let go of other treasures to buy the field in which the treasure of the kingdom is buried (13:44); the dead must be abandoned for the way of life (8:22); entangling riches must be given away to free one for the way of discipleship (19:21). The good news about the reign of God demands conversion.

Reflecting and Recording

Read again the paragraph on page 29 that begins, "We don't reflect enough on the radical change involved in becoming a Christian."

■ ■ ■

Spend some time reflecting on repentance in your life. What "big" occasions of repentance have you experienced? Is repentance an ongoing dynamic in your Christian walk? What specific act of repentance do you need to make today?

■ ■ ■

Write a prayer of repentance and commitment to kingdom living.

During the Day

Continue to read and memorize the Beatitudes.

DAY 6

A Beatitudinal Way of Life

Strive first for the kingdom of God and his righteousness, and all these things will be given to you as well. (Matt. 6:33)

Be perfect. (Matt. 5:48)

The Latin-American Jesuit theologian Jon Sobrino defines *spirituality* as 'profound motivation'. By this, he means those instincts, intuitions, longings, and desires—both of nature and of culture—that move us, inspire us (literally 'breathe through us'), and shape, inform and fill our decisions and actions" (Galloway, *Struggles to Love: The Spirituality of the Beatitudes*, 2).

This definition of spirituality—"profound motivation"—connects with Jesus' charge: "Seek ye first the kingdom of God, and his righteousness; and all these things shall be added unto you" (Matt. 6:33, KJV). Our spirituality is shaped by what we desire most; what we strive for; what motivates us, drives us, moves us to select one priority over another. The primary shaping forces of our life comprise our spirituality.

Jesus calls us to a beatitudinal way of life—a life shaped by the dynamic of seeking and finding God's presence in our life, doing whatever is essential to put God at the very center—or rather, to put ourselves at the very center of God's will.

The word *beatitude* simply means "blessing." On Day 2 we indicated that the word *blessing* comes from two sources—from the Latin word *beatitudo*, which means "consummate bliss," and the Greek word *makarios*, which describes an untouchable joy. To be blessed, then, means receiving a gift that results in deep gladness or bliss. Such bliss is not a frivolous, light kind of happiness but a deep, abiding, life-changing joy.

Jesus says that blessedness is not something we achieve or earn. Blessedness already exists—we enter into the state of blessedness when we seek first the kingdom—when we are poor in spirit, when we mourn, when we begin to live a beatitudinal style of life.

On Day 3, we distinguished between happiness and blessedness, or joy. We don't want to be overly simplistic. As Ralph W. Sockman said:

> To talk about being blessed without being happy is to announce a hymn without starting the tune. Jesus saw and shared [people's] longing for happiness. He did not give them a stone when they asked for bread. He met [people] on the plane of their desires and lifted them to the level of their needs. He filled their dreams with richer and higher happiness. (Sockman, *The Higher Happiness*, 12)

This "higher happiness" is life in the kingdom. Jesus' promise was extravagant: "Seek ye first the kingdom of God and his righteousness; *and all these things shall be added unto you*" (emphasis ours). All these things add up to a happiness the world cannot give or take away. The issue boils down to this: Will we yield ourselves totally to Christ, allow him to shape our lives and give us happiness, or will we continue to seek happiness by pursuing the kingdom of self?

Do you remember your growing-up years—say, when you were five or six? You were old enough to go outside and play. Your mother was not too concerned about what might happen to you. Your neighborhood was safe; there were other children to play with. Those were charming years.

Did you worry about whether you would have any lunch that day? If it was afternoon, did you worry about whether you would have any food on the table at the close of the day? Or did you just play—unconcerned, not worried at all about what would happen next? Most likely you totally immersed yourself in the games, in the fun you were having, in your relationships with your friends.

And then it happened. You would hear a call—"it's lunchtime" or "it's suppertime." And you knew what would happen next. You would leave your play, and food would be ready on the table when you washed your hands and joined the family.

That is the kind of trust and confidence to which Jesus calls us. He desires that we live a beatitudinal lifestyle—a style of life that trusts God to add to our lives the joy and happiness that cannot be taken away.

Reflecting and Recording

We recognize that some readers may not have grown up in a home with loving and protective parents, where there was always a "lunchtime" or a "suppertime." Can you locate in your experience what gave you a sense of security, love, belonging—of being cared for?

■ ■ ■

If you grew up in a warm, loving family, try to imagine what it might have been like not to have that security—and seek to grasp the fullness of a "blessed," beatitudinal way of life.

■ ■ ■

Spend the rest of your time reflecting on this question: Will you yield yourself totally to Christ, allowing him to shape your life and give you happiness, or will you continue to seek happiness by pursuing the kingdom of self?

■ ■ ■

During the Day

Continue to read and memorize the Beatitudes.

DAY 7

Turning the World Right Side Up

We often hear the expression, "She (or he) turned my world upside down." In his teaching, especially in the Sermon on the Mount and particularly the Beatitudes, Jesus turned the world right side up.

He knew the ideas of happiness contained in the Beatitudes would seem foolish to the world. Even his closest disciples, those with whom he sought to share deeply the mysteries of the kingdom, had difficulty understanding his message. How many times had James and John heard Jesus talk about pride and humility? Didn't they hear him say, "Blessed are the meek"? Undoubtedly. Yet, near the end, on their way to Jerusalem where Jesus was going to be tried, condemned, and crucified, they had the gall to request a special place in his kingdom: "Let one of us sit at your right and the other at your left in your glory" (Mark 10:37, NIV).

Can you fathom their dullness of mind? Jesus had told them why he was going to Jerusalem and what would happen there. He would be condemned to death and handed over to people who would mock him and spit on him, flog him and kill him. Three days later, he would rise from death. In that kind of awesome setting, with the profound meaning of all that Jesus was, what he had come to do, and his certainty about how God would raise him from the dead—James and John thought of themselves and the place they wanted to have in his glory. Obviously they had missed the message. Their world was still as it was—not yet turned right side up by Jesus.

Some years ago, the New York Museum of Natural History arranged one room according to a dog's perspective. Table legs looked like huge pillars, chairs resembled lofty thrones, and the mantel above the fireplace appeared to be an unscalable precipice.

Recalling that situation, Ralph Sockman wondered which was reality: a room from the perspective of a dog, or a room as it looks to us? Because we're human, we would answer that a room seen from our perspective is the real one. But here is the rub: might there not be a "divine eye as much above ours in perception as ours is above the dog's?" (Sockman, *The Higher Happiness*, 14).

In the Beatitudes, Jesus gives us the real world of the kingdom. When those Beatitudes prevail in the lives of persons and in society, our world is turned right side up.

Jesus, who turns our world right side up by giving us the Beatitudes, lived them. In him, the characteristics of blessedness can be clearly seen. He was poor in spirit: "Come to me, all you that are weary and are carrying heavy burdens, and I will give you rest. Take my yoke upon you, and learn from me; for I am gentle and humble in heart, and you will find rest for your souls" (Matt. 11:28-29). He mourned—his heart was often broken. He had compassion on the multitude because they were like sheep without a shepherd. He wept over Jerusalem. He hungered and thirsted for righteousness—how many nights did he spend alone in prayer; how often did he seek that quiet place in order to satisfy his hunger for God? He was merciful—so merciful that publicans and sinners were attracted to him. He was pure in heart, always aware of the Father's presence. He was forever making peace, though he was continually persecuted. He turns our worlds right side up because his world was right side up. He can pronounce blessedness upon us in the Beatitudes because he incarnated that blessedness. Paul called Jesus "the divine Yes."

> For the Son of God, Jesus Christ, whom we proclaimed among you, Silvanus and Timothy and I, was not "Yes and No"; but in him it is always "Yes." For in him every one of God's promises is a "Yes." For this reason it is through him that we say the "Amen," to the glory of God. (2 Cor. 1:19-20)

In the days ahead, we will consider specific Beatitudes. Hopefully, we, like Jesus, will become an incarnation of blessedness.

Reflecting and Recording

Pray this prayer:

> Dear Jesus,
> Be present in me in a powerful way today and in the coming days. Possess my mind, heart, and will. Let no word cross my lips that is not your word. Let no thoughts be cultivated that are not your thoughts. Let no deeds be done that are not an expression of your love and concern.
> May your presence be so real in me that others will no longer see me but you, Lord Jesus.
> May I be cheered by your presence and move through these coming days with no hint of anxiety so that your peace may flow from my life. Amen.

If you participate in a group studying this workbook, you will meet sometime today. Picture each person in your group, pray for each one, and ask the Lord to mold the group into a fellowship that will minister to every member.

During the Day

Continue to read and memorize the Beatitudes.

✠

Group Meeting
for Week One

Leader: You will need a dry-erase board or newsprint for this session.

Introduction

Group sessions are most meaningful when all participants talk about their experiences. This guide is designed to facilitate personal sharing. Therefore, you need not be rigid in following these suggestions. The leader especially needs to be sensitive to what is happening in participants' lives and to focus the group's sharing of those experiences in light of that knowledge. Ideas are important; we need to wrestle with new ideas as well as with ideas with which we disagree. The group meeting should not become a debate. Emphasize the experiences and feelings of individuals. While the content of a group study is important, applying the content to our lives and our relationship with God and others needs priority.

As the group begins to talk honestly and openly about what is happening in their lives, group meetings will be more meaningful. This does not mean that group members share only the good or the positive; they can also share their struggles, difficulties, and negatives.

This process of group sharing is not easy; it is deceptive to pretend it is. Growth requires effort. Don't be afraid to share your questions, reservations, and "dry periods," as well as meaningful times.

Sharing Together

1. Begin your meeting by allowing time for each individual to share the most meaningful day with the workbook this week. As leader, begin this sharing. Tell why that particular day was so meaningful.
2. Next, share your most difficult day with the material, describing what you experienced and why it was so difficult.
3. Invite three or four people to share briefly some deed or manner of relating to someone that God may have applauded. Please don't think that such sharing is prideful. It is what John Wesley called Christian conferencing, designed to serve as encouragement and challenge.
4. *Leader:* Write on the board or newsprint the six descriptions of God listed in the Reflecting and Recording section of Day 1. Ask the group, "How many of you have difficulty accepting number 1—ready to forgive?"

Record the number. Go through each description in this fashion, then spend ten to twelve minutes discussing why it is difficult to accept these descriptions of God.

5. Turn to the Reflecting and Recording section of Day 3. Look at the list of situations that often affect our happiness. Invite two or three people to share experiences of joy in their life even during times when they were sad, disappointed, or suffering.

6. Spend eight to ten minutes discussing the difficulty and privilege of putting first things first in relation to occupation, family, relationships with others, and material possessions (Reflecting and Recording, Day 4).

7. Invite someone to read aloud paragraph 4, Day 5, beginning with, "We don't reflect. . . ." Discuss these questions in relation to what is said there:
   a. What new thoughts do you find?
   b. Is there anything you disagreed with? Why?
   c. What might "bearing a cross" in repentance mean?
   d. What behavioral and relational changes may be necessary?

8. Before you move into a time of prayer, ask the group if there is any idea, issue, or question raised in this week's content that they would like to discuss. Spend the remaining time hearing responses from the group.

Praying Together

Each week's suggestions call for the group to pray together. Corporate prayer empowers Christians, and including this dimension in a shared pilgrimage is important.

Group members need to feel comfortable during corporate prayer. No one should feel pressured to pray aloud. Silent corporate prayer may be as vital and meaningful as spoken corporate prayer. Times of silence, when thinking is centered and attention is focused, may provide our deepest periods of prayer.

Verbalizing thoughts and feelings to God in the presence of fellow pilgrims can also be a powerful bonding experience for a group on a common journey. Verbal prayers may be offered spontaneously as persons choose to pray aloud. Avoid suggesting, "Let's go around the circle now, and each one pray."

Suggestions are given each week for this "praying together" time. **Leader,** regard these only as suggestions. What happens in the meeting—the mood, the needs expressed, the timing—should determine the direction of the group's prayer time together. Here are some possibilities for this closing period.

1. Invite the group to spend a few minutes in silence, deliberately thinking about each person in the group and what that person has shared. Offer a silent sentence prayer of petition or thanksgiving for that person.

2. Invite two or three persons to offer a brief, spontaneous prayer, thanking God for the group and for the opportunity to share with others in this study/learning/prayer experience.

3. Encourage everyone to write the names of group members in the front of the workbook and to pray for group members each week. Nothing binds a group together more than mutual prayer.

4. Invite a volunteer to share the prayer of repentance written on Day 5. Then ask the group to pray together the prayer from the Reflecting and Recording section of Day 7.

Week Two

Having Nothing, Possessing Everything

✠

DAY 1

One Diamond with Eight Facets

Blessed are the poor in spirit, for theirs is the kingdom of heaven.
Blessed are those who mourn, for they will be comforted.
Blessed are the meek, for they will inherit the earth.
Blessed are those who hunger and thirst for righteousness, for they will
   be filled.
Blessed are the merciful, for they will receive mercy.
Blessed are the pure in heart, for they will see God.
Blessed are the peacemakers, for they will be called children of God.
Blessed are those who are persecuted for righteousness' sake, for theirs is the
   kingdom of heaven. (Matt. 5:3-10)

Together the Beatitudes describe the character of persons living in the kingdom. There are nine Beatitudes, but because the last two may be combined as one, we often talk about "eight blessings." However, as Archibald M. Hunter reminds us, "we should think not so much of eight different types of character as of one ideal character seen from eight different angles—one diamond with eight facets." (Hunter, *A Pattern for Life*, 34)

As we suggested on Day 7 of last week, the Beatitudes essentially describe Jesus himself:

In the character of Jesus, the distinctive beauties of the Beatitudes harmonize like the colors in a mosaic. He is poor in spirit, a mourner, meek and lowly in heart. He hungers for the supremacy of righteousness, is merciful, pure in heart, the Prince of peace, and suffers for righteousness' sake—yet none of these virtues is cultivated at the expense of another. They blend in his character in their true proportion and express the spirit of perfect love. (Hunter, *A Pattern for Life*, 34)

The blessing named in each Beatitude is comprehensively described as "the kingdom of heaven," which is how the first Beatitude puts it. "Blessed are the poor in spirit, for theirs is the kingdom of heaven." So let's reflect a bit more on the kingdom.

We may think of the kingdom as the totality of salvation—the salvation Jesus brings. Thus, being saved means more than just having a ticket into heaven when we die. It means we have dominion now—ours is the kingdom. As Gregory of Nyssa put it, "He who became poor for us reigns over all creation. Therefore, if you become poor because he became poor, you will also reign because he is reigning." (Gregory of Nyssa in *The Secret of Happiness*, Ruth Connell, comp., 10) Paul captured the dominion that is ours when he made the extravagant claim, "All things are yours, whether . . . the world or life or death or the present or the future—all belong to you, and you belong to Christ, and Christ belongs to God" (1 Cor. 3:21-23).

Salvation, or living in the kingdom, means that we will be comforted in the midst of our mourning. God's mercies are always greater than our troubles. Living in the kingdom means that we will be completely satisfied. We will know wholeness. We realize the promise of Jesus: "I am the bread of life. Whoever comes to me will never be hungry, and whoever believes in me will never be thirsty" (John 6:35).

Living in the kingdom also means mercy—not just now but particularly on the Day of Judgment. One of the great preachers of the ages, John Chrysostom, put it this way: "Mercy imitates God and disappoints Satan." (*The Secret of Happiness*, 25). When we live under God's sovereignty and rule, mercy is the operative dynamic.

Our salvation, living in the kingdom, means confidence; it means the vindication of God's cause. The Crucifixion and the Resurrection give us this confidence. These events demonstrate God's ability to overcome evil with good. Jesus went before us, bearing his cross and dying on that cross so that we might bear our own crosses. Scripture promises that if we share in Christ's death, we will also share in his life. (See Romans 8:17.) If we are with him in his suffering, we will also be with him in his glory.

Salvation means we experience the inevitable joy of becoming children of God and living with God. The Beatitude says, "For they will see God" (Matt. 5:8). The psalmist made the same promise: "They will receive blessing from the LORD, and vindication from the God of their salvation" (Ps. 24:5). As we keep our eyes focused on Jesus Christ, the Son of God, we will see God; we will experience the joy of being children of God.

Reflecting and Recording

Accepting the notion that the Beatitudes describe the character of persons living in the kingdom, spend time reflecting on the following aspects of the meaning of your salvation, or living in the kingdom. To what degree do you experience these aspects of kingdom living?

Comfort in the midst of mourning

■ ■ ■

Mercy now, but especially assurance of mercy on Judgment Day

■ ■ ■

Confidence that evil has been overcome by God's goodness and righteousness. If we share in Christ's suffering, we will also share in his glory.

■ ■ ■

The joy of being a divine heir—living with God

■ ■ ■

Spend the balance of your time pondering this promise: "All belong to you, and you belong to Christ."

■ ■ ■

During the Day

If you have not yet memorized the Beatitudes, continue that process. Seek to move through the day self-consciously as a kingdom person—one who reflects the characteristics of the kingdom.

DAY 2

The Prerequisite for All Blessing

Though we would not say that one Beatitude is more important than another, the order of the Beatitudes has significance. "Blessed are the poor in spirit, for theirs is the kingdom of heaven." It is no accident that this Beatitude is first. Poverty of spirit comes first because it must be first; it is the foundation for the house of spiritual character.

It is the rich soil in which alone other graces will grow and flourish. Hilltops are barren, because the soil is washed off by the rains; but the valleys are fertile because there the rich deposits gather. In like manner proud hearts are sterile, affording no soil in which spiritual graces can grow; but lowly hearts are fertile with grace, and in them all lovely things grow. If only we are truly poor in spirit, our life will be rich in its fruits. (J. R. Miller, *The Master's Blesseds*, 36)

The Beatitudes as we have them are in Greek. The Greek word used to translate Jesus' Aramaic word for *poor* is a severe one. It is *ptochos*, which means absolute and complete poverty. William Barclay helps us with a word study to give the significant meaning of that severe word. In Greek, there are two words for *poor*, according to Barclay. One word is *penes*, which describes persons who have to work for a living, people serving their own needs with their own hands. *Penes* describes working persons, those with nothing superfluous, persons who are not rich but also are not destitute.

The other word is *ptochos*, which describes "absolute and abject poverty." Barclay says it is connected with the root *ptossein*, which means "to crouch or to cower," and it describes "the poverty which is beaten to its knees." (Barclay, *The Gospel of Matthew*, rev. ed., 1:90)

Comparing the two words helps us plumb the depths of this Beatitude. *Penes* describes someone who has nothing superfluous; *ptochos* describes someone who has nothing at all.

Barclay gives a more complete meaning by studying the Hebrew words for *poor*, which are *'ani* and *ebion*:

These words in Hebrew underwent a four-stage development of meaning. (i) They began by meaning simply *poor*. (ii) They went on to mean, *because poor, therefore having no influence, or power, or help, or prestige*. (iii) They went on to mean, *because having no influence, therefore down-trodden and oppressed by men*. (iv) Finally, they came to describe *the man who, because he has no earthly resources whatever, puts his whole trust in God*. (Barclay, *The Gospel of Matthew*, rev. ed., 1:91)

So, in Hebrew the word *poor* was used to describe the humble and helpless person who put all of his or her trust in God. (Barclay, *The Gospel of Matthew*, rev. ed., 1:91)

Combining the study of words, Barclay translates "Blessed are the poor in spirit" like this: "Blessed is the [person] who has realised his [or her] own utter helplessness, and who has put his whole trust in God." (Barclay, *The Gospel of Matthew*, rev. ed., 1:91)

The Gospels of Matthew, Mark, and Luke include a story that illumines this Beatitude:

As [Jesus] was setting out on a journey, a man ran up and knelt before him, and asked him, "Good Teacher, what must I do to inherit eternal life?" Jesus said to him, "Why do you call me good? No one is good but God alone. You know the commandments: 'You shall not murder; You shall not commit adultery; You shall not steal; You shall not bear false witness; You shall not defraud; Honor your father and mother.'" He said to him, "Teacher, I have kept all these since my youth." Jesus, looking at him, loved him and said, "You lack one thing; go, sell what you own, and give the money to the poor, and you will have treasure in heaven; then come, follow me." When he heard this, he was shocked and went away grieving, for he had many possessions. (Mark 10:17-22)

We don't believe that this man's money kept him out of the kingdom. Instead, the cause was his feeling of self-sufficiency—his attitude that he'd done everything necessary. He had kept the commandments and therefore could do whatever was necessary for salvation. He was not poor in spirit; he had not placed his whole trust in God.

Compare this man to Paul the apostle who had the right cultural and religious résumé:

- born into a pure-blooded Jewish family, of the tribe of Benjamin;
- circumcised when he was eight days old;
- a Pharisee who strictly obeyed the Jewish law (Phil. 3:5).

Paul had the credentials. "If others have reason for confidence in their own efforts, I have even more!" he said (3:4, NLT). "I once thought these things were valuable, but now I consider them worthless . . . when compared with the infinite value of knowing Christ Jesus my Lord" (vv. 7-8, NLT).

Reflecting and Recording

Barclay translated this first Beatitude, "Blessed is the [one] who has realised his [or her] own utter helplessness, and who has put his whole trust in God." Name three people you think are "poor in spirit" according to this understanding.

Compare yourself to each of these persons. What are the most significant differences between you and them? Make some notes here.

During the Day

If you have not yet memorized the Beatitudes, continue that process. At different times during the day, in various relationships and while performing your work, deliberately examine whether you have any sense of helplessness and/or whether you are putting your whole trust in God.

DAY 3

Begin Low If You Would Build High

Down in Perry County, Mississippi, we had a saying: "His learning has gone to his head." Of course learning is in the head—it's in the mind. But everybody knew what we were talking about: Someone had gotten an education and had become intoxicated with his newfound knowledge. Thinking she was smarter than other folks, she became impressed with her own achievement. He had become convinced of his own importance but wasn't too aware of what was going on around him—especially with other people.

We used that phrase not only in relation to learning but in other areas as well: "His position has gone to his head." "Getting that last promotion went to her head." It became a distortion. Perhaps getting an education should have given meaning; being promoted to a new position could have provided happiness and satisfaction—and there's nothing wrong with that. But pride becomes distorted when it causes one to think more highly of himself than he ought—or to think that her position and achievements put her in a higher place than those around her.

J. B. Phillips's translation of the first Beatitude is helpful: "How happy are the humble-minded, for the kingdom of Heaven is theirs." Being humble-minded in our world is not easy. We have been taught to be self-reliant, independent, and resourceful; to be sharp thinkers and intellectually confident. We are taught to put no limit on what we think we can do.

A story in Luke's Gospel speaks to us here:

[Jesus] also told this parable to some who trusted in themselves that they were righteous and regarded others with contempt: "Two men went up to the temple to pray, one a Pharisee and the other a tax collector. The Pharisee, standing by himself, was praying thus, 'God, I thank you that I am not like other people: thieves, rogues, adulterers, or even like this tax collector. I fast twice a week; I give a tenth of all my income.' But the tax collector, standing far off, would not even look up to heaven, but was beating his breast and saying, 'God, be merciful to me, a sinner!' I tell you, this man went down to his home justified rather than the other; for all who exalt themselves will be humbled, but all who humble themselves will be exalted." (Luke 18:9-14)

Jesus exalts the tax collector in the story because the tax collector realized his need for God's mercy—he was humble-minded. The Pharisee made the mistake of comparing himself with others, rather than with God's standard of righteousness. He thanked God that he was not like other people. Instead of being humble-minded, he was filled with pride. His self-assurance and self-satisfaction were so blatant that he missed God's mercy. Like the Pharisee, we do not claim the gospel of love but compare ourselves to others. We manipulate life into an acceptable pattern that we can control.

J. C. Ryle reminds us: "Humility is the very first letter in the alphabet of Christianity. We must begin low if we would build high." (Connell, comp., *The Secret of Happiness*, 8)

A bit of paradox exists here. I remember going through a tough time in my leadership of Asbury Theological Seminary. Much of the difficulty revolved around financial issues. The national economy had gravely impacted our endowment income. I felt helpless and went through three or four weeks of near despair. The secret of my overcoming was the discovery of the difference between *resignation* and *surrender*. Resigning myself to circumstances was unhealthy and unChristian. Resignation is passive and negative. In contrast, surrender to the Lord in the midst of, even in spite of, circumstances is positive and active.

As I was learning that lesson, I wrote in my journal one morning: "I'm poor in spirit. I'm willing to be 'brought low,' to be humbled by seeing how inadequate all our resources, wisdom, and strength are and how dependent we are upon God. But I'm not willing to give up trusting that God will prevail—and if we are faithful, God will provide."

Lloyd Ogilvie, a Presbyterian minister and former chaplain of the U.S. Senate, wrote a challenging word about our spiritual poverty:

> Many of us do not realize our poverty of spirit because we are not living an adventurous enough life. We aren't living courageously enough to have any other invisible means of support than Christ. Once we get involved with people and their needs, and really care about them, we will soon find that we do not have adequate patience or persistence. People try, test, and trouble us if we dare to care. Whenever we try to change social conditions, we meet obstacles of closed minds and resistant wills. Then we realize how poor in wisdom we are. We do not realize our poverty of spirit until we accept the potential challenge in which we are to live out our faith. (Ogilvie, *God's Best for My Life*, reading for June 11)

Reflecting and Recording

Recall and describe here an experience when you felt totally inadequate and found strength and meaning in surrender and dependence on the Lord.

As you look at your present situation and your immediate future, is there a potential challenge that, if you accept it, will call for such faith and commitment that you will realize how "poor in spirit" you are? Name that challenge in prayer and commit yourself to accepting it and responding in surrender and dependence.

■ ■ ■

What does the notion that we must "begin low if we would build high" say to your present life situation?

■ ■ ■

During the Day

If you have not yet memorized the Beatitudes, continue that process. Continue your effort of deliberately examining whether in your various relationships and work you have any sense of helplessness and/or whether you are putting your whole trust in God.

DAY 4

Restoration of God's Image

To be poor in spirit is to recognize that we are utterly helpless to save ourselves—even to receive the forgiving grace of God for our justification.

Simply to see salvation totally as God's unmerited gift of justification is a limited understanding. Certainly that is a part of salvation, and we do experience deep guilt because we "fall short" of the glory of God. (See Romans 3:23.) Thus, a crucial aspect of salvation is forgiveness of sin. But we find an equally central biblical theme in Romans 7–8, in which Paul makes clear that the deep impact of sin in our lives is spiritual debilitation: "Even though the desire to do good is in me, I am not able to do it" (Rom. 7:18, GNT). Therefore, salvation means the ongoing gracious gift of God to empower us and provide a transforming presence within our lives.

One of the assertions of the Christian faith is that we are created in God's image. We're made in God's image, and we are created for God. We do not fulfill our nature—who we were created to be as human beings—apart from the experience of God's presence in our lives.

It is the work of God to draw us into communion; it is human nature to resist God. This is a part of what we mean when we talk about *original sin*. We ignore who we are and our destiny of growing into God's image. This is what sin is all about: our love turns into self-love. In his letter to the Romans, Paul says that we exchange "the truth about God for a lie" (Rom. 1:25). Thus, the image of God within us is distorted.

It's a struggle and a paradox that eventuates in the confession of Saint Paul: "For I do not do the good I want, but the evil I do not want is what I do. . . . Wretched man that I am! Who will rescue me from this body of death?" (Rom. 7:19, 24). The image of God is marked upon us, yet sin keeps God at a distance. Salvation, then, is more than simply being saved from sin and given a guarantee of heaven; it means the restoration of the *imago dei* (the image of God) in us. John Wesley called this dynamic *sanctification*.

Poverty of spirit is required for our sanctification—that is, for our having God's image restored within us and for living from that powerful dynamic of knowing that through God's initiative we belong to God and we are to live in God's presence. Only the poor in spirit are aware enough of their condition to keep that dynamic of sanctification at work.

John Wesley wrote a marvelous passage describing the twofold nature of grace—comprised of God's mercy and power:

By "the grace of God" is sometimes to be understood that free love, that unmerited mercy, by which I, a sinner, through the merits of Christ, am now reconciled to God. But in this place it rather means that power of God the Holy Ghost which "worketh in us both to will and to do of his good pleasure." As soon as ever the grace of God (in the former sense, his pardoning love) is manifested to our soul, the grace of God (in the latter sense, the power of his Spirit) takes place therein. And now we can perform, through God, what to [ourselves] was impossible. . . .

I rejoice because he gives me to feel in myself "the mind that was in Christ" . . . a renewal of soul after his likeness." ("Sermon 12: The Witness of Our Own Spirit," in *Sermons I*, 1–33, ed. Albert C. Outler, *The Works of John Wesley*, 1:309–10)

God's grace is manifested in us to shape us into the likeness of Christ. We live out our sanctification through our character disposition and outward actions, with God's grace shaping our character into the likeness of Christ, and our outward action reflecting that commitment. To be poor in spirit is to know our need for mercy and power that, as Wesley said, we may go on to salvation, to sanctification, to the wholeness of God's image being restored in us.

Reflecting and Recording

Wesley's word, quoted above, is packed with meaning. In order to grasp it fully, paraphrase the passage in your own words, writing in the space beside it.
Spend the remaining time pondering this truth: Salvation means God's ongoing gracious gift to empower us and provide a transforming presence in our lives.

■ ■ ■

During the Day

Seek someone to talk with about your beginning study of the Beatitudes. Share a low-key witness of your experiences, especially about being poor in spirit.

DAY 5

Not Poverty of Material Things

Most of us do not know real poverty. I thought I did. Born in 1934, I grew up in Perry County, Mississippi. The Great Depression really didn't end in the South until World War II. My father was a laborer, working at all sorts of jobs:

cutting logs for timber; cutting pulpwood to make paper; working in what we call "the stump woods"; and finally, to some degree, moving up in the world by taking a trade course in welding—and working as a welder in the shipyards during and after the war.

We lived in a three-room house with no indoor plumbing. We owned a small piece of ground; therefore, we raised a lot of our food. We didn't have much of this world's goods, but we never went hungry. People around us in that part of the South were far below the poverty line as we would think of that measurement today. It wasn't until I got to high school that I consciously thought I was poor. I was emotionally ravaged by that notion. Then in 1968 I went to India, Thailand, Africa, and the Middle East, and I began to get a taste of real poverty.

Pulitzer prize–winning author Rick Bragg has written a marvelous book titled *All Over but the Shoutin'*. It's part memoir, part confession, as he tells the story of growing up dirt-poor in northeastern Alabama. I identified with Bragg because I had experienced what he wrote about. Seemingly destined for either the cotton mills or the penitentiary, he instead became a reporter for the *New York Times*. He courageously tells the story of his family and their poverty, concluding:

> The only thing poverty does is grind down your nerve endings to a point that you can work harder and stoop lower than most people are willing to. It chips away a person's dreams to a point that the hopelessness shows through, and the dreamer accepts that hard work and borrowed houses are all this life will ever be. While my mother will stare you dead in the eye and say she never thought of herself as poor, do not believe for one second that she did not see the rest of the world, the better world, spinning around her, out of reach. (Bragg, *All Over but the Shoutin'*, 25)

Most of us do not know real poverty. And many of us are seduced by the notion that you do not miss what you never had. That's a lie! Being poor does not blind you to the riches around you. The fact that you live in a house you don't own—even a hovel—does not mean you don't dream of a house of your own.

Jesus does not bless that kind of poverty in this first Beatitude. He is not talking about poverty in one's worldly condition. To be sure, Jesus was gentle in his attitude toward those whose earthly condition was hard. In Luke's Gospel, the Beatitude simply reads, "Blessed are you who are poor" (6:20), without any qualification.

Scripture attests to the truth that God has taken a preferential option on behalf of the poor. Jesus said he had been anointed to preach the gospel to the poor, and when John's disciples came to Jesus requesting some evidence that he might be the Messiah, he responded to them that the gospel was preached to the poor.

A huge part of Christ's glory was his friendship with the poor. As Christians today, in our role as what Martin Luther called "little Christs," we must not fail Jesus in his interest in, compassion for, and commitment to the poor. But, as we have said, that's not what this Beatitude is about—it's not about poverty in terms of one's worldly condition. We must be careful not to think that this Beatitude calls material poverty a good thing. We all know that poverty is not good; we know what it does to people. Jesus would never have called people who don't have enough to eat, who barely have a shelter over their head, who have inadequate clothing—he would not call that kind of poverty blessed. In fact, part of his mission was to proclaim the release of captives—those who were captives to economic systems that deprived them of the basic needs of life.

While Luke simply says, "Blessed are you who are poor," Matthew says, "Blessed are the poor *in spirit*" (emphasis ours). As we have already discussed, the poor about whom Jesus is speaking are those who, out of desperate need, knowing themselves completely inadequate to save themselves, cast themselves wholly on God for their salvation.

Carlo Carretto gives us a good perspective on poverty in his first-person biography of Saint Francis of Assisi. In it Francis says:

And when I thought of the poor I had met in my life, especially in recent years, it was clear that there were poor who were only poor—very sad, often angry, and certainly not blessed.

And then again, I recalled very well, there were poor people who were quite otherwise, poor people who wore their poverty beautifully.

Poor people who had the conviction that they were being guided by God, supported by his Presence.

Poor people who were able to love, in spite of their sudden vexations— poor people who were patient in trial, rich in hope, strong in adversity.

Poor people who were blessed because they could bear witness, every day, that God was present in their lives, and that he provided for them as he did for the sparrows of the sky, which possess no granaries.

Yes, this captivated me.

To bear witness, to testify, to myself and to other human beings, that God alone sufficed for me, and that I did not have to be concerned about anything, anything at all—"think of the flowers of the field; they never have to spin or weave; yet not even Solomon in all his regalia was like one of these" (Luke 12:27).

The thought of being fed, clothed, and guided by God . . . uplifted me. No power on earth could have persuaded me to change my mind. Putting a little money aside—keeping a larder—buying a house—for me this would have meant a lack of trust in my Lord.

Oh, I would not have proposed this manner of life for everyone. For example, it would not have been the thing for my father.

That would have been impossible. Society had other laws. People had different callings.

I was proposing it for myself, as I wished to be a witness of God's love. And I would have proposed it for those who would follow me. (Carretto, *I, Francis*, 19)

Reflecting and Recording

Do you know a poor person you would identify as poor in spirit? Describe that person here.

Do you know a reasonably wealthy person you would identify as poor in spirit? Briefly describe that person.

Spend a few minutes comparing these two persons. How are they alike? How are they different?

■ ■ ■

Though Saint Francis chose a life of material poverty for himself and others, he would not propose his manner of life for everyone, for he said, "People had different callings." He chose it for himself, "as I wished to be a witness of God's love." Spend some time considering how we can give witness to God's love without choosing a vocation of poverty.

■ ■ ■

Close your time by praying the prayer attributed to Saint Francis:

> Lord, make me an instrument of your peace;
> where there is hatred, let me sow love;
> where there is injury, pardon;
> where there is doubt, faith;
> where there is despair, hope;
> where there is darkness, light;
> and where there is sadness, joy.
>
> O Divine Master, grant that I may not so much seek
> to be consoled as to console;
> to be understood as to understand;

to be loved as to love;
for it is in giving that we receive;
it is in pardoning that we are pardoned;
and it is in dying that we are born to eternal life. Amen.

During the Day

Think about what this day will demand of you as a part of your everyday responsibilities. Plan some act of mercy to carry out during the next twenty-four hours.

The prayer attributed to Saint Francis is printed on page 213. Cut it out and carry it with you. Over the next few days, find two or three occasions each day to pray it.

DAY 6

Serving the Poor as a Means to Becoming Poor in Spirit

Do not store up for yourselves treasures on earth, where moth and rust consume and where thieves break in and steal; but store up for yourselves treasures in heaven, where neither moth nor rust consumes and where thieves do not break in and steal. For where your treasure is, there your heart will be also. (Matt. 6:19-21)

Amos Wilder, a renowned New Testament scholar, says the ethics of the Beatitudes have less to do with obedience than with grace. (Wilder, *Eschatology and Ethics in the Teaching of Jesus*, 120, quoted in Hunter, *A Pattern for Life*, 35) God through Jesus Christ is the gracious giver, and we are to be humble receivers. We do not seek to live by the Beatitudes in order to deserve or win some reward or divine approval. Rather, blessedness comes to us because we claim no merit for ourselves; we know in our hearts our deepest needs; we are confident and content in resting wholly on the mercy of God.

If poverty of spirit means to be totally dependent, to be bereft of anything that would cause us to be self-sufficient, then Christians must think seriously about money and the possession of material goods. In his Sermon on the Mount, Jesus said, "Where your treasure is, there your heart will be also." Just before he said this, he had told a parable of what it means to keep the commandments and to inherit the kingdom of heaven. He concluded that parable by saying, "It is easier for a camel to go through the eye of a needle than for a rich person to enter the Kingdom of God!" (Matt. 19:24, NLT).

Indeed, material wealth can be a stumbling block in our relationship to God. John Wesley wrote: "I fear, wherever riches have increased . . . the essence of religion, the mind that was in Christ, has decreased in the same proportion." (Wesley, in *The Methodist Societies: History, Nature, and Design*, ed. Rupert E. Davies, *The Works of John Wesley*, 9:529).

Wealth can also be a resource for meeting human needs. Back in 1996, George Gallup Jr. wrote a book titled *The Saints among Us*. In an address at Asbury Theological Seminary, Gallup spoke about lessons he had learned from the polling out of which the book grew. A major finding was that true holiness is seen most vividly in seemingly ordinary people—poor, marginally educated, and the majority of them nonwhite. Gallup spoke about the implication of this discovery in an interview in *America*:

> In many cases there are people who have known dire economic straits, yet their trust has enabled them to step outside their grim conditions and to find joy in life, so they run against the grain. The fact that they are downscale suggests that though they are burdened by economic problems, they are not overcome by them. They are more forgiving, more grateful, and more likely to be unprejudiced, as well as twice as likely to be involved in outreach to neighbors, as persons at the lower end of the spiritual commitment scale. In other studies we have done, such as financial giving, we found that the poor give a larger proportion of their income to charity than the rich. Being surrounded by misery, they see opportunities to help on every side. The rich, especially now, with the widening gap between rich and poor, have a tendency to cordon themselves off and therefore don't see much of the grimness of life. (George M. Anderson, "Talking about religion: an interview with George H. Gallup, Jr.," *America*, October 26, 1996: 20, quoted in Brennan Manning, *Ruthless Trust*, 28)

The safest route for a wealthy person is to use his or her wealth as a resource for meeting the needs of the poor. When we see that our wealth competes with our devotion to the Lord, we must confess that our wealth is a stumbling block and acknowledge the truth of Jesus' teaching: "Where your treasure is, there your heart will be also" (Matt. 6:21).

Doesn't it make sense that serving the poor can become a dynamic means of grace enabling us to recognize our poverty of spirit? Yet we need to keep our service in perspective. We usually think of serving the poor or other acts of compassion as duties we must perform, as requirements from God, or simply as ways of helping others. To be sure, all of this is true. But a greater issue related to being poor in spirit is the need to engage ourselves in works of mercy, not simply for the sake of others but also for our own sake. These acts of mercy we perform are practices God has designed to empower us. They give us the mind of Christ, and they shape us as Christians.

Nothing—not even what we would normally call works of piety—prayer, worship, scripture study—shapes us into the likeness of Christ so much as works of mercy. It's not enough simply to give money to the poor. Compassion means that we must identify with, relate to, and have a relationship with the poor. Wesley was blatantly assertive about this. He emphasized visiting the sick and needy even more than giving them money or offering them aid. He knew that being with the sick and the needy plays a significant role in making us compassionate people, those who emulate the compassion of Christ.

A negative poverty of spirit can be seen in some people who are ungenerous and unthankful. They may or may not have wealth, yet they diminish other people with their attitudes and actions. In doing so, they diminish themselves. Their spiritual sensitivity shrinks. In contrast, true poverty of spirit comes from the honest awareness that our material wealth or our natural strength and resources do not bring ultimate meaning. No matter how extensive our resources, they do not provide the satisfaction our hearts demand. So, poor in spirit and confessing our inadequacy, we turn to God, who graciously responds, compensating for our weaknesses and making available to us tremendous resources.

As we lean upon God completely, gradually perhaps but *progressively* learning the secrets of self-denial and dependence, we become poor in spirit and inheritors of the kingdom. We hold our material possessions in wise perspective and use them to bless the poor, which in turn blesses us.

Reflecting and Recording

Spend some time reflecting on Amos Wilder's claim that the ethics of the Beatitudes have less to do with obedience than grace.

■ ■ ■

In your own words, express Wilder's claim in two or three sentences.

Spend three to four minutes examining yourself in response to this question: To what degree does my wealth or lack of wealth serve as a stumbling block in my relationship with God?

■ ■ ■

Carlo Carretto says, "God is simple and we make him complicated. He is close to us and we think him far away. . . . The true secret of making contact with God is littleness, simplicity of heart, poverty of spirit: all the things that pride, wealth, and cleverness foil in us." (Carretto, *I Sought and I Found: My Experience of God and of the Church*, trans. Robert Barr, 18)

Carretto identifies three qualities as the secret to making contact with God:

1. littleness

2. simplicity of heart

3. poverty of spirit

He says that pride, wealth, and cleverness prevent the expression of these characteristics in our lives. In the space provided above, make some notes about whether Carretto is right about these things in light of your situation, and how you might change.

Close your time with this prayer:

Lord, today and in the days ahead, show me what it means to be little, in other words, simple in heart and poor in spirit. Give me the will and the strength to live in this manner.

During the Day

Did you perform the act of mercy you planned yesterday? Instead of planning today, determine to remain open to any opportunity to act mercifully.

DAY 7

Having Nothing, Possessing Everything

We are treated as impostors, and yet are true; as unknown, and yet are well known; as dying, and see—we are alive; as punished, and yet not killed; as sorrowful, yet always rejoicing; as poor, yet making many rich; as having nothing, and yet possessing everything. (2 Cor. 6:8-10)

We have argued that we're not to think of the first Beatitude as affirming material poverty. Nor are we to think of it as affirming anything that would look like "poor spiritedness" or low self-esteem.

The poor in spirit are small in their own eyes, honest about their weakness and struggles, and open to constructive criticism. Jesus' counsel to take the last place does not shock them because they know they belong there. Unfortunately, however, this sense of self can become self-pitying, self-condemning abjectness that expresses itself as low self-esteem. It is not the same as the "gentle and humble in heart" (Matt. 11:29) Jesus claimed as his own. Jesus lived for God in utter self-forgetfulness, enthralled with God and living securely in the acceptance of the One with whom he lived so intimately that he addressed as "Abba," Father.

So, following Jesus, the "poor in spirit" do not confuse humility with low self-esteem or self-pity. They know they are loved, accepted, and forgiven. What we need is a humility that does not count itself humble. We're not poor in spirit because we're poor-spirited but because we feel our spiritual need.

In all of life, especially in the context of the Christian faith, we are all beggars. We know that the gospel is not for the proud and the self-sufficient. Rather, it is for those who acknowledge and own their insufficiency, limitation, and sinfulness and cast themselves on the mercy of God in Jesus Christ.

The apostle Paul gives us this paradox as one of the foundational principles of the Christian life. The description is a dramatic one: "having nothing, and yet possessing everything." The New Living Translation renders this description as, "We are poor, but we give spiritual riches to others. We own nothing, and yet we have everything" (2 Cor. 6:10, NLT).

How much energy we waste in the vain effort to gain material possessions! We expend energy trying to gain not only material wealth, but, as Hannah Whitall Smith reminds us,

> Some strive to get possession of certain experiences, some seek after ecstatic feelings, some try to make themselves rich in theological views and dogmas, some store up a long list of works done and results achieved, some seek to acquire illuminations or to accumulate gifts and graces. In short, Christians, almost without exception, seek to possess a store of something or other, which they fancy will serve to recommend them to God and make them worthy of his love and care. (Smith, *God Is Enough*, 14)

But Jesus says, "Blessed are the poor in spirit," and Paul says that when we are most Christian, we "have nothing but possess everything." It's obvious that the one thing God wants is for us to empty ourselves of all our *own* possessions so that we will depend upon God for everything. Our problem is that we trust Jesus with *some* things some of the time when we need to trust him with *all* things all of the time.

That's what Jesus is talking about, the kind of spirit that remains aware of its own utter lack of resources to meet the challenges of daily living—the spirit that finds help and strength in God through the presence of Jesus Christ.

Here is a modern-day rewording of Jesus' prescription for a life well-lived:

> You're blessed when you're at the end of your rope. With less of you there is more of God and his rule.
>
> You're blessed when you feel you've lost what is most dear to you. Only then can you be embraced by the One most dear to you.
>
> You're blessed when you're content with just who you are—no more, no less. That's the moment you find yourselves proud owners of everything that can't be bought. . . .
>
> You're blessed when you can show people how to cooperate instead of compete or fight. That's when you discover who you really are, and your place in God's family. (Matt. 5:3-5, 9, *The Message*)

In contrast to Jesus' teaching, we hear subtle or not-so-subtle cultural messages like, "Happiness comes when you reach the top," or "The person with the most toys wins." The world seeks to convince us that we have to "keep up with the Joneses," that appearance is everything, and that it doesn't matter whom you hurt in your struggle to get to the top.

The unfortunate reality is that when we follow the world's blueprint for success and happiness, more often than not we end up discovering not happiness but stress and insignificance. Jesus provides us with an alternative, where happiness becomes an unexpected yet deep and abiding consequence of living a grace-filled life, in sync with God and with an openness to others.

Reflecting and Recording

Read again the cultural messages the world would have us believe. To what degree have you believed these messages and felt any of the above situations would bring you happiness?

■ ■ ■

Spend a few minutes reflecting on "poor-spirited." To what degree does this adjective describe you? What is the difference between "poor-spirited" and "poor in spirit"?

■ ■ ■

On Day 2 you were asked to name three persons who are poor in spirit. Consider those persons. Is anyone wealthy? Is anyone poor? Is anyone known for a superior intellect? Is anyone in a position of significant social, economic, religious, or cultural influence? What do the characteristics of these persons say to you about being poor in spirit?

■ ■ ■

If you participate in a group studying this workbook, pray for group members and your time together today. Close your time by praying the prayer suggested yesterday (p. 60).

■ ■ ■

During the Day

Hopefully you have memorized the Beatitudes. Find three or four occasions today to repeat them to yourself. And, if the occasion arises, discuss your involvement in this Beatitude study with someone; ask that person to share insights on the first Beatitude.

✠

Group Meeting
for Week Two

Introduction

Participation in a group such as the one studying this book involves a covenant relationship. You will profit most from daily use of this workbook if you faithfully attend weekly meetings. Do not feel guilty if you have to miss a day in the workbook or discouraged if you cannot give the full thirty minutes in daily discipline. Don't hesitate to share any difficulties with the group. We learn something about ourselves when we share our thoughts and feelings with others. You may discover, for instance, that you are subconsciously afraid of dealing with the content of a particular day because its requirements might reveal something about you. Be patient with yourself and always remain open to what God may be seeking to teach you.

Your spiritual growth, in part, hinges upon your group participation, so share as openly as you can and listen to what others say. If you are attentive, you may pick up meaning beyond the surface of their words. Participating sensitively in this fashion is crucial. Responding immediately to the feelings you discern is also important. At times the group may need to focus its entire attention upon a particular individual. If some need or concern is expressed, the leader may ask the group to enter into a brief period of special prayer. But participants should not depend solely upon the leader for this kind of sensitivity. Even if you aren't the leader, don't hesitate to ask the group to join you in special prayer. This praying may be silent, or someone may wish to lead the group in prayer.

Remember that you have a contribution to make to the group. Even if you consider your thoughts or experiences trivial or unimportant, they may be exactly what another person needs to hear. You need not seek to be profound but simply to share your experience. Also, if you happen to say something that is not well received or is misunderstood, don't be defensive or critical of yourself or others. Don't get diverted by overly scrutinizing your words and actions. Saint Francis de Sales said, "It is self-love which makes us anxious to know whether what we have said or done is approved or not." (Connell, comp., *A Year with the Saints*, 209)

Sharing Together

Leader: Time may not permit you to use all the suggestions each week. Select what will most benefit your group. Be thoroughly familiar with these suggestions so that you can move through them selectively according to the direction in which the group is moving and according to the time available. Plan ahead, but do not hesitate to change your plan in response to the sharing taking place and the needs that emerge.

1. Open your time together with the leader offering a brief prayer of thanksgiving for the opportunity of sharing with the group and with petitions for openness in sharing and loving responses to one another.

2. Spend eight to ten minutes giving those who wish a chance to share their most meaningful or most difficult day this week.

3. Turn to the Reflecting and Recording section of Day 1. Five aspects of kingdom living are listed there. Go through them one by one, asking persons to respond in terms of their own experience: "How have you experienced this aspect of kingdom living?" Get a witness/response to each—if possible. If there is not a personal response to any one of these, spend a few minutes discussing why this may be so.

4. Invite two volunteers to share their description of a person they named on Day 2 as being poor in spirit.

5. Spend ten to twelve minutes discussing the difference between *resignation* and *surrender* as discussed on Day 3. Invite persons to share experiences of inadequacy, then of finding strength and meaning in dependence on the Lord.

6. Read aloud paragraph 4 of Day 4 (p. 49), beginning, "It is the work . . ." Spend eight to ten minutes discussing this statement: "This is what sin is all about: our love turns into self-love."

7. Invite someone to read his or her paraphrase of Wesley from Day 4. Then spend six to eight minutes discussing this statement: "Salvation means the ongoing gracious gift of God to empower us and to provide a transforming presence in our lives."

8. Spend ten to twelve minutes discussing this statement: "God has taken a preferential option on behalf of the poor." Talk about how, if this statement is true, we need to change personally, and how the congregation of which we are a part might respond. Also talk about how our material wealth or lack of material wealth may be a stumbling block in our relationship to God.

9. Invite someone to describe a poor person who is poor in spirit, and another to describe a wealthy person who is poor in spirit. (Reflecting and Recording, Day 5)

10. Read aloud the words from Hannah Whitall Smith, Day 7, page 40. Spend the balance of your time discussing her claims and the notion that we empty ourselves of our own things so that we can depend on God for *everything*.

Praying Together

1. Praying corporately each week is a special ministry. Take time now for a period of spoken prayer. Allow each person to mention any special needs he or she wishes to share with the entire group. A good pattern is to ask for a period of prayer after each need is mentioned. The entire group may pray silently, or someone may offer a brief two- or three-sentence spoken prayer.

2. Close your time by praying aloud together the prayer attributed to Saint Francis from pages 53–54.

Week Three

Tears in the Night,
Joy in the Morning

DAY 1

Strange Bedfellows

It's a strange notion to think of entering the house of sorrow to look for joy. Sadness and happiness don't normally share the same room. In most people's experience, mourning is the opposite of rejoicing. In the vernacular, we would say sorrow and joy are strange bedfellows. Yet, Jesus said, "Blessed are those who mourn."

Jesus couldn't possibly mean that all who mourn are blessed. Where is the blessedness in poor parents grieving because they lack food for their hungry children? Where is the blessedness of people in a war-torn land who see no hope for their own survival and the survival of their family? It's not difficult to call to mind those who suffer, but it is difficult to see how God's blessing fits in. So, what is Jesus talking about in this Beatitude?

Sorrow and tears are part of life. The ability to cry is a gift of God. Why do some parents say to their sons, "Big boys don't cry"? How many men shrivel up in their emotional expression because they're too macho to cry?

The Bible talks about all kinds of sorrow and mourning, and it certainly makes the case that weeping and mourning are a part of life. In fact, the Bible uses twenty Hebrew words and thirteen Greek words to express sadness and grief. Mourning is a natural human response. On all sorts of occasions in the Psalms the writer expresses grief over God's absence:

> My soul thirsts for God, for the living God.
> When shall I come and behold the face of God?
> My tears have been my food day and night,
>   while people say to me continually,
> "Where is your God?" (Ps. 42:2-3)

One of the Bible's beautiful stories of tears can be found in Luke 7. A woman comes in from the street, interrupts a dinner party, and washes Jesus' feet with her tears, drying them with her own hair. Her tears are tears of heartfelt gratitude, devotion, and worship.

There are tears of loneliness. The psalmist cries out, "My soul thirsts for you, my body longs for you, in a dry and weary land where there is no water" (Ps. 63:1, NIV).

There are tears of loss. Abraham wept when his wife, Sarah, died (Gen. 23:2). Mary Magdalene wept because Jesus was dead—hers were the deep, sad tears of loss, releasing the terrible pain in her heart. Others who had been with Jesus "were mourning and weeping" after his death. (Mark 16:10)

There are tears of love. Jesus wept at the grave of Lazarus because he loved Lazarus. (John 11:35) He wept over the city of Jerusalem because he loved its people. (Luke 19:41)

These kinds of mourning are natural and good. Certainly those who mourn because of loneliness, loss, and love will be comforted. Jesus said, "Come unto me, all you that are weary and are carrying heavy burdens, and I will give you rest" (Matt. 11:28). The Gospel of Matthew presents Jesus as the fulfillment of the second Beatitude. He is the one who took on the sins of the world, embracing the world in all its brokenness and mourning. (1:21; 8:17). Thus he was able to cure all who were still under the authority of this world's alienation. Jesus fulfilled the messianic promise of the prophet Isaiah:

> The spirit of the Lord GOD is upon me,
>   because the LORD has anointed me;
> he has sent me to bring good news to the oppressed,
>   to bind up the brokenhearted,
> to proclaim liberty to the captives,
>   and release to the prisoners;
> to proclaim the year of the LORD's favor, and the day of vengeance of our God;
>   to comfort all who mourn;
> to provide for those who mourn in Zion—
>   to give them a garland instead of ashes,
> the oil of gladness instead of mourning,
>   the mantle of praise instead of a faint spirit.
> They will be called oaks of righteousness,
>   the planting of the LORD, to display his glory. (Isa. 61:1-3)

Those are powerful words: to comfort all who mourn, to place on those who mourn in Zion a garland instead of ashes, to give them the oil of gladness in place of mourning, a glorious mantle instead of a listless spirit.

So Jesus not only gives us the Beatitude, he becomes the fulfillment of the Beatitude.

Reflecting and Recording

Beside each designation of the cause for tears, make some notes about an occasion of your own tears brought on by the designated circumstances:

the absence of God

heartfelt gratitude

tears of loneliness

tears of loss

tears of love

Look over the causes for grief. Do you know persons who mourn because of one of these circumstances? Write their names in the margin beside the cause, and spend a few minutes praying for each one.

Spend the balance of your time reflecting on the claim that Jesus not only gives us this Beatitude, but he fulfills it. In what way have you found this to be true?

During the Day

When you see someone who appears sad, offer a brief but immediate prayer for that person. In addition, pray specifically, by name, for the persons you listed above.

DAY 2

Our Cross: Mourning

Yesterday we mentioned that the Bible contains numerous Greek and Hebrew words for sadness and grief. Barclay reminds us the Greek word used for *mourn* in the second Beatitude is the strongest word for mourning in the Greek language.

> It is the word which is used for mourning for the dead, for the passionate lament for one who was loved. . . . It is defined as the kind of grief which takes such a hold on a [person] that it cannot be hid. . . . Here then is an amazing kind of bliss: Blessed is the [person] who mourns like one mourning for the dead. (Barclay, *The Gospel of Matthew,* rev. ed., 1:93)

Donald English, in his preaching, expressed truth in this fashion: "You'll always meet God in the world as suffering, dying love. . . . You will know that suffering, dying love is the way in which God lovingly feels his way through the affairs of the world in order that the result might be the very best result for everybody involved." (*Proceedings of the Fifteenth World Methodist Conference, Nairobi, Kenya, July 23–29, 1986,* ed. Joe Hale, 196)

The Gospel writers were convinced that if we are going to see Jesus, we have to see him on the cross—vulnerable and weak. If we are going to be his disciples, we must seek to live in solidarity with him, to share in the fellowship of his suffering. Paul understood this clearly:

> Yet whatever gains I had, these I have come to regard as loss because of Christ. More than that, I regard everything as loss because of the surpassing value of knowing Christ Jesus my Lord. For his sake I have suffered the loss of all things, and I regard them as rubbish, in order that I may gain Christ and be found in him, not having a righteousness of my own that comes from the law, but one that comes through faith in Christ, the righteousness from God based on faith. I want to know Christ and the power of his resurrection and the sharing of his sufferings by becoming like him in his death, if somehow I may attain the resurrection from the dead. (Phil. 3:7-11)

Paul had one passion: to know Christ. He realized that knowing Christ involved the cross for himself. He wrote, "I want to know Christ and the power of his resurrection and the sharing of his sufferings by becoming like him in his death" (Phil. 3:10). The concept of sharing Christ's suffering became such a radical part of Paul's life that he never ceased talking about it. He wrote to the Colossians, "Now

I rejoice in what was suffered for you, and I fill up in my flesh what is still lacking in regard to Christ's afflictions, for the sake of his body, which is the church" (Col. 1:24, NIV). The idea that we can share Christ's suffering is strange and somewhat confusing. Some may charge Paul with thinking that somehow Christ's suffering was insufficient for human sin and that he (Paul) had to do something about that. That's not the issue at all.

There is nothing deficient in Christ's offering of himself as a reconciling act. What Paul expresses is what he sought to live out as the deepest desire of his life: to join in the *fellowship* of Christ's suffering. He called for the pattern of Christ's own saving work to be incorporated into the life of every Christian. Paul hoped that we would reproduce that kind of passion, that willingness to suffer, to give ourselves in a cross-style of life: *a life of mourning.*

Francis de Sales, one of the saints with whom I've kept company through the years, wrote a memorable passage about our relationship to the cross. He said, "Kiss frequently the crosses which the Lord sends you . . . without regarding of what sort they may be." Now consider this statement (also from de Sales):

> The merit of crosses does not consist in their weight, but in the manner in which they are borne. (Connell, comp., *A Year with the Saints*, 115)

Does that sound like a strange notion? "Kiss frequently the crosses which the Lord sends you." If we can get beyond the strangeness of the image, we will discover this truth: We are to welcome the suffering that comes into our lives as an invitation to love and trust God more. We will mourn and make our suffering an extension of the suffering of Christ.

What cross in your life do you need to kiss?

- the cross you bear for a child caught in the chains of a destructive addiction
- disabled parents for whom you are having to care
- an unsatisfying job that appears to be the only means of survival for your family
- being a single parent because an irresponsible, uncaring spouse left you
- the call to serve the poor
- a life of chastity as a single person

What cross in your life do you need to kiss?

The big question is this: Are we willing to give ourselves for the sake of others and for the world? As the bread and wine of Holy Communion are the body of Christ broken for us and his blood poured out on our behalf, so Christ would want us to be the bread broken for the sake of the world and the blood poured out for the salvation of others.

That can't happen without our willingness to mourn on behalf of others.

Reflecting and Recording

Go back in the text to the question "What cross in your life do you need to kiss?" A series of "crosses" is listed. Read the list, putting a check (✓) to the left of those you might need to "kiss."

Examine your life further. Is there a "cross" or crosses in your experience not listed that you need to kiss? Make notes here.

Return to the list of "crosses" in the text. Read them again, thinking of persons you know. Who bears one of these crosses or some other heavy burden? List those persons here.

Spend the rest of your time praying for those you have listed and offering your own "cross" or crosses to Jesus, the One who promised comfort for our mourning.

During the Day

Yesterday you were asked to pray for particular persons during the day. Today you have identified others for whom you might pray. The following prayer is printed on page 211. Cut it out and carry it with you during the coming days. Write the names of persons you have identified in the blanks, and call their names in prayer.

Gracious God,
as your Son wept with Mary and Martha at the tomb of Lazarus,
look with compassion on those who grieve, [especially *Name(s)*].
Grant them the assurance of your presence now and faith in your
    eternal goodness,
that in them may be fulfilled the promise
    that those who mourn shall be comforted;
through Jesus Christ our Lord. Amen.
(Laurence Hull Stookey, "For Those Who Mourn," *The United Methodist Hymnal*, No. 461)

✠

DAY 3

The Treasury of Comfort

The great Christian writer and thinker C. S. Lewis equated love with vulnerability. We cannot love, he said, without risking a wounded or even broken heart. If we want to keep from being hurt, then we must wrap up our heart with little pamperings and luxuries and avoid involvement with others. "You must give your heart to no one," he wrote, "not even to an animal." (Lewis, *The Four Loves*, 121)

When God offered love to the world in the person of Jesus, God didn't try to protect Godself or hold anything back. In risk-taking love, God became vulnerable, giving Godself completely in love to us as Jesus, ending up on a cross. Jesus held nothing back; he loved unconditionally. His second Beatitude suggests that there are heights of dependence most of us have not yet reached. We can trust that Jesus was confident in his word when he said, "Blessed are those who mourn, for they will be comforted." Jesus wept over Jerusalem. He grieved deeply over the death of his friend Lazarus. He was filled with compassion and deep sorrow for the people because they were "like sheep without a shepherd" (Mark 6:34).

It becomes obvious, when we look at our heavenly Father and our Savior, Jesus, that *great lovers make great mourners*. The greater the love, the greater the loss, and the greater the mourning. When there is little love, there is little loss.

Interestingly, the deeper the cavern that pain carves in our spirit, the more joy we can contain. Fred Van Tatenhove, a professor at Asbury Theological Seminary, provides a vivid witness to this truth. He retired early to care for his wife, who had progressive supranuclear palsy, an incurable disease that gradually destroys one's ability to command one's muscles.

I received a letter from Fred soon after he made this decision to care for Janet. In that letter, he told me about how the disease was working and would continue to progress in Janet's life:

> Janet is no longer able to do anything for herself. She can't turn over in bed or move her muscles by choice. We use a wheelchair to move from place to place. Two weeks ago she had to have a feeding tube inserted, since she could hardly swallow, and when she did, food was getting into her lungs. I feed her a liquid supplement four times a day. That is going well. Progressive supranuclear palsy destroys all ability to use muscles. Since there is no treatment, she will eventually be confined to her bed.

Eventually Janet became bedridden, and Fred continued to love and care for her for two and a half years until she died. In response to my prayers and support after Janet's death, Fred wrote:

> I've come to understand something about grief, at least in my loss. When I was losing Janet a little every month for two and a half years, there would be times when I would have to go out of her presence to experience that loss. But each time when I returned to care for her, it meant I would experience more losing. Now I do not feel grief for her in her illness but only when I look at pictures of her or remember her as healthy. Then I feel what I have lost, but I do not return to her and more losing. So the grief now has a wonderful sense of healing. I thank God for His comfort and grace.

Janet died at home with Fred and her son, Greg, at her side, a nurse, and her daughter, Jana, on the speaker phone. Fred said, "Her illness had spoken, but God had the final and eternal word. I would never wish for her to struggle any longer. She is at rest, and I feel a deep loss but also a *comforting peace.*"

A couple of months after Janet's death, I visited with Fred. His spirit had a lightness about it. He talked joyously about Janet and their life together. I doubt that Fred could have shown such joy if pain and loss had not carved such a deep cavern in his spirit. When I left Fred that day, I reread the letter he had written to me. One paragraph said:

> This past year I kept a quote on my computer that reads, "Life is not measured by the number of breaths you take but by the moments that take your breath away." Janet was always one of those special "moments" for me. That quote also reminded me to live each day with Janet with appreciation and love.

Fred lived with his pain, which carved a deep cavern in his spirit. But now that cavern is filled with joy—joy that comes from his memories but also joy that comes because he can live out the lessons he learned from his pain and sorrow.

Could it be that Jesus placed this Beatitude, "Blessed are those who mourn, for they shall be comforted," immediately after his emphasis on the poor in spirit because he wanted to say to us that when all seems lost and our resources are utterly worthless, he has an unlimited treasury of comfort waiting to share with us? The experience of folks like Fred seems to suggest that this is so.

Suffering is hard to accept and impossible to understand. But when you add to it the kind of love Fred demonstrated, it becomes an almost unfathomable mystery. Thinking about Fred and Janet, I remember a hymn we used to sing in the country church in which I grew up. Its chorus said:

> By and by, when the morning comes,
> when the saints of God are gathered home,
> we'll tell the story how we've overcome,
> for we'll understand it better by and by.
> (Charles Albert Tindley, c. 1906, *The United Methodist Hymnal,* No. 525)

Such was the confidence of the psalmist when he wrote, "Weeping may linger for the night, but joy comes with the morning" (Ps. 30:5).

Reflecting and Recording

Recall and describe an experience (your own or the experience of someone you know) that reminds you of the psalmist's confident statement, "Weeping may linger for the night, but joy comes with the morning."

Spend some time attentively examining the following statements:

When there is little love, there is little loss.

■ ■ ■

The greater the love, the greater the loss and the greater the mourning.

■ ■ ■

The deeper the cavern that pain carves in our spirit, the more joy we can contain.

■ ■ ■

During the Day

Continue using the prayer suggested yesterday.

DAY 4

Out of the Great Tribulation

After this I looked, and there was a great multitude that no one could count, from every nation, from all tribes and peoples and languages, standing before the throne and before the Lamb, robed in white, with palm branches in their hands. They cried out in a loud voice, saying,

> "Salvation belongs to our God who is seated on the throne, and
> to the Lamb!"

And all the angels stood around the throne and around the elders and the four living creatures, and they fell on their faces before the throne and worshiped God, singing,

> "Amen! Blessing and glory and wisdom and thanksgiving and honor
> and power and might be to our God forever and ever! Amen."

Then one of the elders addressed me, saying, "Who are these, robed in white, and where have they come from?" I said to him, "Sir, you are the one that knows." Then he said to me, "These are they who have come out of the great ordeal; they have washed their robes and made them white in the blood of the Lamb." (Rev. 7:9-14)

It's a beautiful picture: the redeemed of the Lord gathered around the throne, singing praises to God. Among them are some very special people who appear to have a special glory. They're described as a multitude that could not even be counted. Wearing white robes and carrying palms in their hands, they come from all the nations of the world and have a place of special honor before the throne. Who are these favored ones? Where have they come from?

They have come out of the great tribulation. They're a joyous multitude who have passed through the deep valley of sorrow and suffering. Their baptism has been one of tears. Their robes are washed in the blood of the Lamb, so they bear the emblem of victory. Isn't this vision of John in the Revelation a great commentary on Jesus' Beatitude, "Blessed are those who mourn"?

Included in Jesus' meaning for *mourning* is the deep sorrow we experience because of our sins. Christians witness to this in different ways. John Wesley had lived a disciplined Christian life, according to his misunderstanding at the time. He spent time in Georgia as a missionary to the Indians but was a failure there and returned to England in a deep depression. He said he experienced a "continual sorrow and heaviness." "I feel," he said, "that 'I am sold under sin.' I know that I too deserve nothing but wrath, being full of all abominations." Shortly after this confession, he experienced a conversion that he described in these words:

> I felt my heart strangely warmed. I felt I did trust in Christ, Christ alone for salvation; and an assurance was given me that he had taken away *my* sins, even *mine*, and saved *me* from the law of sin and death. (*The Works of John Wesley*, vol. 19, *Journal and Diaries I: 1735–38*, eds. W. Reginald Ward and Richard P. Heitzenrater, 241–42, 250)

Mourning for sin was a very real experience for Wesley—and it is a genuine experience that countless others have discovered. Salvation comes when we begin to feel deep sorrow for our sins. This sorrow leads to genuine repentance.

We're not too prone to think about what our sin does to God, yet our sin separates us from God—and this alienation grieves the heart of God. If only we could get a glimpse of the effect of our sin on God, we would truly mourn. God's deepest desire is to have fellowship with us.

The book of Genesis describes how God feels about our sin:

> The LORD saw that the wickedness of humankind was great in the earth, and that every inclination of the thoughts of their hearts was only evil continually. And the LORD was sorry that he had made humankind on the earth, and it grieved him to his heart. (Gen. 6:5-6)

The New Living Translation renders verse 6 like this: "So the Lord was sorry he had ever made them [humans]. It broke his heart."

Jesus knew that if we ever caught a glimpse of what sin does to God, we would mourn. Our mourning would lead to confession and repentance. Our confession and repentance lead to forgiveness and the joy of reconciliation. James, that stern apostle, exhorts his readers to "let there be tears for the wrong things you have done. Let there be sorrow and deep grief. Let there be sadness instead of laughter, and gloom instead of joy" (James 4:9, NLT). Then he added, "When you bow down before the Lord and admit your dependence on him, he will lift you up" (v. 10, NLT).

It doesn't matter whether our sins are great or relatively small; all sin is an affront to God, breaking God's heart. Ultimately all sin is against God, and until we deal with it, we remain separated from God and in distress. The Holy Spirit works in our lives to convince us of this truth, and when convinced, we're deeply sorry; we repent, and the joy of forgiveness comes. Our joy is the delight of being forgiven.

Reflecting and Recording

Many scholars believe that David wrote Psalm 51 as a prayer of confession and repentance after his sin of committing adultery with Bathsheba and having her husband killed. Reflecting on his sin, he said:

Have mercy on me, O God, according to your steadfast love;
   according to your abundant mercy blot out my transgressions.
Wash me thoroughly from my iniquity,
   and cleanse me from my sin.
For I know my transgressions, and my sin is ever before me. (Ps. 51:1-3)

In verses 10-12, he continues:

Create in me a clean heart, O God,
   and put a new and right spirit within me.
Do not cast me away from your presence,
   and do not take your holy spirit from me.
Restore to me the joy of your salvation, and sustain in me a willing spirit.

Reflect on your life. Do you have unconfessed sins? broken relationships? persons you have sinned against? Have you repented of every known sin? Is there someone to whom you need to confess? As you think about your life, pray aloud David's petitions from Psalm 51 (vv. 1-3, 10-12).

■ ■ ■

During the Day

Continue praying the intercessory prayer from Day 2 (p. 70).

DAY 5

Godly Sorrow

Now I rejoice, not because you were grieved, but because your grief led to repentance; for you felt a godly grief, so that you were not harmed in any way by us. For godly grief produces a repentance that leads to salvation and brings no regret, but worldly grief produces death. For see what earnestness this godly grief has produced in you, what eagerness to clear yourselves, what indignation, what alarm, what longing, what zeal, what punishment! At every point you have proved yourselves guiltless in the matter. (2 Cor. 7:9-11)

It is interesting that the second Beatitude, which promises comfort, follows the first Beatitude, with its blessing on the poor in spirit. The quality of our mourning relates to all of our life. Not all sorrow is a blessing. The sorrow produced by injured pride refuses to be comforted. When our possessiveness is thwarted and we see ourselves as oppressed, the resulting sorrow will not be comforted. When our pride is injured and we grieve about losing prestige, that kind of grief will not receive the comfort of Christ.

Paul identified *godly grief* as the kind of grief that will be blessed. In 2 Corinthians, Paul talks about three kinds of sorrow. The first kind of sorrow is the deep sorrow the Corinthians felt for him because of their concern. This sorrow is blessed and forms a dimension of intercessory prayer. When our concern becomes so pronounced that we have sorrow for another, the sorrow itself becomes our prayer. We are "poor in spirit" and we *mourn* because we know we are helpless. We have to trust God completely. Often our sorrow is so deep and our helplessness so evident that we can't even verbalize our prayer. Paul summarizes our condition:

> Likewise the Spirit helps us in our weakness; for we do not know how to pray as we ought, but that very Spirit intercedes with sighs too deep for words. And God, who searches the heart, knows what is the mind of the Spirit, because the Spirit intercedes for the saints according to the will of God. (Rom. 8:26-27)

This is one form of godly sorrow: deep concern and care for another.

Paul also talked about the sorrow that *produces a repentance leading to salvation*. This is the sorrow we considered yesterday. When we realize that God loves us so much that anything that separates us from God or others is of grave concern to God, then we experience sorrow. The cross serves as a constant reminder of how deeply God loves and cares for us. We look at the cross and see the tears of God because more than anything else, the cross reminds us that our sin breaks God's heart.

Godly sorrow comes when we are in touch with God, begin to feel what God feels, and become disturbed by what disturbs God. Likewise, blessedness is being in touch with the heart of God, delighting in what God delights in, and seeking God's will for ourselves and others.

The third kind of sorrow Paul mentions is *worldly sorrow*. He says, "Godly grief produces a repentance that leads to salvation and brings no regret, but worldly grief produces death."

Worldly sorrow means we are preoccupied with ourselves and our happiness. What makes us happy at a superficial level—having things go our way, not being bothered or troubled, being successful? It's a good exercise simply to ask ourselves what we regret. Our regrets reveal much about our priorities. We need to think about what worldly sorrow is most of the time: self-pity.

Brennan Manning has written a life-transforming book called *Ruthless Trust*. It's a very personal, autobiographical look at one of the most important dimensions of the Christian life: trust. Through pain and joy, through ecstasy and tragedy, Manning has arrived at that rock-bottom trust and invites us to share in it. He shows us how true, radical trust in God can transform our lives. His title, *Ruthless Trust*, is revealing within itself. Webster defines the adjective *ruthless* as "without pity." Manning says, "I use the word, in this context of trust, to mean 'without self-pity' because self-pity is the arch-enemy of trust." (Manning, *Ruthless Trust*, 164)

Tears of self-pity are not the kind of mourning Jesus describes as blessed. But since self-pity is such a part of our lives, we need to keep it in perspective. Manning writes:

> When pain and suffering intrude and our secure, well-regulated lives are blown apart, when tragedy makes its unwelcome appearance and we are deaf to everything but the shriek of our own heartache, when courage flies out the window and the world around us suddenly seems dark and menacing, self-pity is the first, normal, unavoidable, and probably right reaction; and we only exhaust ourselves further if we attempt to suppress it. . . .
>
> However, there comes a time when self-pity becomes malignant, seducing us into self-destructive behavioral patterns of withdrawal, isolation, drinking, drugging, and so forth. We simply ask for the grace to set a time limit on our self-pity. (Manning, *Ruthless Trust*, 164)

But this does not mean that self-pity has to go. It simply has to be kept in perspective. It can become the kind of mourning that leads us to God and an utter dependence upon God.

Morrie Schwartz, a Brandeis University sociology professor, contracted ALS (Lou Gehrig's disease), a progressive neurodegenerative disease. People with ALS lose their ability to walk, speak, swallow, and breathe, yet in most cases the mind remains unaffected. The disease is usually fatal within two to five years. One of Schwartz's former students, Mitch Albom, wrote *Tuesdays with Morrie*, a book that tells the story of his love for his mentor. Every Tuesday, Albom flew from Detroit to Boston to spend the day with his teacher. One day, he asked Morrie if he ever felt sorry for himself.

> "Sometimes, in the mornings," he said. "That's when I mourn. I feel around my body, I move my fingers and my hands—whatever I can still move—and I mourn what I've lost. I mourn the slow, insidious way in which I'm dying. But then I stop mourning."
>
> Just like that?
>
> "I give myself a good cry if I need it. But then I concentrate on all the good things still in my life. On the people who are coming to see me. On the stories I'm going to hear. On you—if it's Tuesday. Because we're Tuesday people."
>
> I grinned. Tuesday people.
>
> "Mitch, I don't allow myself any more self-pity than that. A little each morning, a few tears, and that's all." (Albom, *Tuesdays with Morrie*, 56–57)

Reflecting and Recording

Is there a person for whom you hold great concern—a godly sorrow? In your imagination, see Jesus embracing that person, speaking to that person's need. Hold that picture in your mind for a few moments.

■ ■ ■

List two or three events or situations during the past two or three months that you regret.

Are these regrets "worldly sorrow"? Do they relate to your own satisfaction and happiness? Are they *worthy* regrets?

Spend the balance of your time reflecting on this word by Martyn Lloyd-Jones:

> If we truly mourn, we shall rejoice, we shall be made happy, we shall be comforted. For it is when [we see ourselves] in this unutterable hopelessness that the Holy Spirit reveals unto [us] the Lord Jesus Christ as [our] perfect satisfaction. (Connell, comp., *The Secret of Happiness*, 14)

■ ■ ■

During the Day

Be sensitive to twinges of regret that may come today—regrets that reflect *worldly* sorrow. Ask the Lord to give you godly sorrow instead.

✠

DAY 6

The Cross: The Mourning of God

What then are we to say about these things? If God is for us, who is against us? He who did not withhold his own Son, but gave him up for all of us, will he not with him also give us everything else? Who will bring any charge against God's elect? It is God who justifies. Who is to condemn? It is Christ Jesus, who died, yes, who was raised, who is at the right hand of God, who indeed intercedes for us. Who will separate us from the love of Christ? Will hardship, or distress, or persecution, or famine, or nakedness, or peril, or sword? (Rom. 8:31-35)

Calvary demonstrates the mourning of God. What a world of meaning can be found in that one assertion: "God did not keep back his own Son, but he gave him for us" (v. 32, CEV). The cross serves as a constant reminder of the depth of God's love.

We grasp for analogies to explain who God is and how God relates to us. Some people are artists, but God is the greatest artist. Some are wise, but God is wisdom itself. When we run out of analogies, we say that God is love, because love is the best thing we know. How, then, do we talk about the love of God? We're not likely to say God loves us like a lover but rather that God loves us like a parent. While romantic love dazzles, parental love wins the prize for endurance. When we have seen heroic love, most likely it has been the love of a parent for a child. Parents love in the face of contempt; they continue to give despite ingratitude; they keep vigil and hope despite rejection. If fallible human beings can sometimes demonstrate such love, God's love must be even greater.

Instead of exacting payment from us for all the sins we have committed, all the times we have gone astray, and the many times we have messed up in life—instead of exacting a payment from us, God pays the price. God becomes human in Jesus and lays down his own life out of love for us. God's love *is* greater.

True blessedness is being in touch with the heart of God, seeking to feel what God feels, to be disturbed by what disturbs God, to have our hearts broken by what breaks God's heart. God loves us so much that anything that separates us from God or others gravely concerns God. God weeps when we hurt ourselves or others.

So, when we mourn, we feel the pulse of the loving, forgiving heart of God. Not only individuals but also the church, the corporate body of Christ, must claim this truth. Congregations need to be aware and confess that they have disappointed and wounded people. If this statement surprises you, talk to a pastor or therapist. He or she will tell you of wounded persons who have left the church because they felt unwelcome. Many have been wounded by the world and come to church, expecting better treatment. We live in a world in which it is easy for people to be hurt, and not all hurts are the same. The church, as the body of Christ, is to be a healing community—a community that mourns for the wounded and becomes a place of comfort, restoration, and reconciliation.

In a confronting and challenging article in *Christianity Today*, Tim Stafford identified wounds that require the church's awareness.

1. *Abused people*. The Catholic Church's recent scandals offer many examples, but Catholic priests aren't alone. Protestant leaders, too, make improper sexual advances, misuse funds, or abuse their authority. Some people can shrug this off and "get over it." Others cannot. . . .

2. *Neglected people*. We live in a bureaucratic, impersonal world, and people are desperate to be noticed and cared for. . . .

Pastor and writer Eugene Peterson says, "People come to church expecting to have their lives taken seriously, God taken seriously, and they're thrown into this secularized entertainment mode. They are not taken seriously as souls." . . .

3. *Lonely people*. Modern society is full of people looking for love. Some come from broken or dysfunctional families, and they hope the church will offer warmth they never found at home. Churches often seem to promise exactly what they hope for. Psychologist Larry Crabb [writes], "People are aware as never before of their longing for community, for encounters with a supernatural God, for reality beneath the mess. They go to church thinking this is going to happen, but the deepest need of their soul is missed." . . .

4. *Guilt-laden people*. Though we live in a "guiltless society," stripped of all the old moralisms, many people today are still weighed down by guilt, some of it deserved, some of it not. . . .

5. *Overinvolved people*. Churches attract idealists. Almost inevitably, some idealists become overinvolved, overidentifying themselves with their ministries. Burnout can become a psychic and spiritual wound that lasts long after the original fatigue. (Stafford, "The Church's Walking Wounded," *Christianity Today* [March 2003]: 67–68)

Stafford closes his article with a pressing challenge:

What people want and what they need are not the same. Their expectations may be impossible, and their neediness endless. We may help them more by challenging them to serve others than by trying to fill their empty holes.

Still, I can't help remembering that Jesus showed impatience only toward those who defined themselves as healthy—never toward those in pain. He identified his mission with the lost sheep, and with those in need of healing. When such people accosted him in the street, he stopped for them. He never lost sight of his larger agenda, but he always stopped for them. (Stafford, "The Church's Walking Wounded," *Christianity Today* [March 2003]: 69)

Certainly, Jesus' meaning of mourning in this Beatitude is more than grief at the loss of a loved one. It encompasses a deep sorrow for our sins, which, as we indicated yesterday, leads to confession, forgiveness, and the joy of reconciliation. It also in this profound sense means feeling God's heart of forgiving love for others. The comfort we receive is in the joy of the forgiveness that is ours—the delight that is ours in being forgiven. That joy is so profound, so deep, so overwhelming that we seek to become vessels that let God's love flow into the hearts of others.

Reflecting and Recording

Spend a few minutes reflecting on this statement: "Calvary demonstrates the mourning of God."

■ ■ ■

Name persons you know who fit in the following categories:

abused people

neglected people

lonely people

guilt-laden people

overinvolved people

How can you or your congregation minister to these persons?

Spend the rest of your time allowing this truth to permeate your consciousness: "True blessedness is being in touch with the heart of God, seeking to feel what God feels, to be disturbed by what disturbs God, to have our hearts broken by what breaks God's heart."

■ ■ ■

During the Day

Call or write one or more of the wounded persons you named above. Seek to assure them that "those who mourn will be comforted."

DAY 7

The God of All Comfort

Blessed be the God and Father of our Lord Jesus Christ, the Father of mercies and the God of all consolation, who consoles us in all our affliction, so that we may be able to console those who are in any affliction with the consolation with which we ourselves are consoled by God. For just as the sufferings of Christ are abundant for us, so also our consolation is abundant through Christ. If we are being afflicted, it is for your consolation and salvation; if we are being consoled, it is for your consolation, which you experience when you patiently endure the same sufferings that we are also suffering. Our hope for you is unshaken; for we know that as you share in our sufferings, so also you share in our consolation. (2 Cor. 1:3-7)

We are blessed when we weep over our own sins because our awareness of sin and deep sorrow for our sins leads to repentance and confession, which in turn lead to forgiveness and reconciliation. So, we're blessed when we weep over our own sin. We are equally blessed when we weep over the sins of others. There is no happiness, no joyous blessedness like knowing we are accepted and loved. When we know such acceptance and love, we want everyone else to experience it.

In a profound sense, mourning also means feeling God's heart of forgiving love for others. We weep over what people do to us and to themselves. We're comforted when forgiveness and reconciliation come between us and others, as well as when we become instruments for others to receive God's forgiving love—whether or not we're personally involved with them.

I am very much in touch with my most profound experience of mourning. Despite what appears to be a most successful ministry, my wife, Jerry, and I have known deep pain and struggle. I have wrestled with my role and performance as a father. I have found myself measuring my identity and worth by my performance, not just as a professional minister but as a parent. My son, Kevin, has had a roller-coaster life—a twenty-year battle with addictions. Praise God, he is becoming "more than a conqueror" through Christ who loves him. We're so excited about that. But the struggle, frustration, and deep pain have, at times, been almost unbearable. The resulting fear and sense of failure have issued often in an ongoing agonizing prayer: "Oh God, please! I want to be a good father. What is it that I need to do? Show me what sacrifices I need to make to be a good father, to play a redemptive role in my son's life."

Many things have happened in that relationship and in Kevin's journey, as well as Jerry's and my journey in relation to him. Kevin gave me permission to share this story. We reached a climactic moment in our relationship in 2000. I was attending General Conference and was involved in the critical issues—or what I believed were the critical issues—facing The United Methodist Church. A Christian counselor with whom Kevin was working called to tell me she thought it was absolutely necessary for Kevin and me to have some time together—the sooner the better. He had reached a pivotal point in his own spiritual journey, and she felt that our meeting was essential. I left General Conference late one afternoon, arrived in Memphis in the middle of the night, and went to bed but slept very little, knowing that I would see Kevin the next morning. Again, I was praying, "Oh God, I want to be faithful to you and to Kevin. I want to be a good father. I want Kevin to know how much I love him. I want to be accountable, and I want him to be accountable."

When I arrived at Kevin's apartment the next morning, he was in the shower. He shouted that he would be out in just a minute. When he came out, he had a basin of water and a towel and told me he wanted to wash my feet to show how much he loved me. I responded, "I want to wash your feet and show you how much I love you." So, for about an hour we washed each other's feet and cried and prayed together as we shared our love.

The experience of washing my son's feet and having him wash mine was just as important as my call to be the president of Asbury Seminary or my call to any other positions I've held in the church. As much as anything else in my life, that experience clarified my knowledge that my identity does not lie in anything I do or any success I've had. I'm certain that I don't have to be the best father in the world; I don't have to be the best president Asbury Seminary has ever had; I don't have to pastor a six-thousand-member church; I don't have to *be* anything but someone who is centered in God, constantly cultivating a relationship with God and seeking to live from an identity that has found its center and rest in God.

Deep comfort comes out of our mourning when we are reconciled to God, but it also comes when we are reconciled to another person from whom we have been estranged.

I have one final thought as we reflect on the second Beatitude: this Beatitude makes the case that nothing need be wasted; everything we experience can serve God's plan.

The psalmist gave witness to this truth:

Forever, O Lord, your word stands firm in heaven.
Your faithfulness extends to every generation,
    as enduring as the earth you created.
Your laws remain true today, for everything serves your plans.
If your law hadn't sustained me with joy, I would have died in my misery.
I will never forget your commandments,
    for you have used them to restore my joy and health. (Ps. 119:89-93, NLT)

The psalmist was not stating an untested truth. He confessed, "I faint with longing for your salvation" (v. 81, NLT); "I am shriveled like a wineskin in the smoke" (v. 83, NLT); "These arrogant people . . . have dug deep pits for me to fall into" (v. 85, NLT). The psalmist did not escape the dark problems, nor could he comprehend the deep mysteries of life, but he was confident of God's faithfulness "to every generation." He overcame by his trust, his certainty that everything we experience can serve God's plan.

Reflecting and Recording

Recall and record here a personal experience of mourning for a loved one from whom you felt estranged or who was separated from God. If reconciliation has taken place, register that; if not, simply express briefly your continuing mourning.

Reread Psalm 119:89-93, and spend a few minutes giving deliberate attention to this thought: Nothing need be wasted; everything we experience can serve God's plan.

■ ■ ■

During the Day

Call or write one or two persons you listed yesterday or prayed for on Days 1–4.

Group Meeting for Week Three

Introduction

Two essential ingredients for a Christian fellowship are feedback and follow-up. Feedback keeps the group dynamic working positively for all participants. Follow-up expresses Christian concern and ministry.

The leader is the one primarily responsible for feedback and can elicit it by encouraging all members to share their feelings about how the group is functioning. Listening is crucial. Listening to one another, as much as any other action, affirms others. When we listen to another, we say, "You are important; I value you." Being sure we understand the meaning of what others say is critical too. We often mishear. "Are you saying _____?" is a good question to check what we heard. If a couple of persons in a group listen and give feedback in this fashion, they can set the mood for the whole group.

Follow-up is a function for everyone. If we listen to what others say, we will discover needs and concerns beneath the surface, situations that deserve special prayer and attention. Make notes of these as the group shares. Follow up during the week with a telephone call, an encouraging note, or maybe a visit. The distinguishing quality of Christian fellowship is caring in action. Ideally, our caring should be so evident that others notice and remark, "My, how those Christians love one another!" One expression of the "mourning" Jesus said would be blessed is godly sorrow—a deep concern and care for one another. We show this care and concern by attentively listening and lovingly responding to others.

Saint Augustine said, "All our good and all our evil certainly lies in the character of our actions. As they are, so are we; for we are the tree, and they the fruit, and therefore, they prove what each one is." (*A Year with the Saints*, 227) Follow up each week with others in the group.

Sharing Together

By this time persons are beginning to feel safe in the group and perhaps more willing to share. Still, there is no place for pressure. Be sensitive to those who are slow to share. Coax them gently. Every person is a gift to the group.

1.   Begin your time together by singing a familiar chorus or verse of a hymn.

2. Spend eight to ten minutes letting each participant talk about "how I'm doing" with this workbook. What is positive? What is negative? Are there special meanings, joys, or difficulties? Encourage one another.

3. Invite the group to turn to the Reflecting and Recording section of Day 1. Occasions and circumstances of grief are listed there. Invite willing persons to share in response to each category. Seek to get at least one person to talk about each designation of "the cause for tears." Allow twelve to fifteen minutes for this sharing.

4. Spend four or five minutes discussing what it means to "kiss frequently the crosses which the Lord sends you."

5. Invite two or three people to share what cross in their life they need to kiss.

Leader: Someone may share such a deep concern that you will want immediately to pray for the person yourself, invite someone else to do so, or simply have a couple of minutes of silent prayer for the person and/or circumstance that has been presented to the group.

6. Spend a few minutes discussing this claim: "The merit of crosses does not consist in their weight, but in the manner in which they are borne."

7. Invite one or two persons to share an experience that verifies the promise of the psalmist: "Weeping may linger for the night, but joy comes with the morning."

8. Invite someone to read aloud the last paragraph of Day 4 (just before Reflecting and Recording). Then spend eight to ten minutes discussing it. Do we believe that all sin is sin against God? How do we think about "small" and "big" sin as it affects our relationship to God? Do some "sins" separate us from God more than others? What is repentance all about?

9. Invite someone in the group to read the paragraph on page 78 that begins, "Tears of self-pity are not. . . ." Then spend six to eight minutes discussing the meaning of worldly sorrow and self-pity and why this is not blessed by Jesus.

10. Spend eight to ten minutes discussing the ministry of your congregation. How does the congregation respond to abused people? neglected people? lonely people? guilt-laden people? overinvolved people? Are our hearts and the hearts of those in our congregation broken by what breaks God's heart?

11. Close your time of sharing by giving as many persons as wish to share some experience that verifies this Beatitude, "Blessed are those who mourn, for they will be comforted."

Praying Together

William Law said the following about spiritual disciplines:

Reading is good, Hearing is good, Conversation and meditation are good; but then they are only good at Times and Occasions. . . . But the Spirit of Prayer is for all Times, and all Occasions; It is a Lamp that is to be always burning, a Light to be ever shining; every Thing calls for it, every Thing is to be done in it, and governed by it because it is, and means, and wills nothing else, but the whole Totality of the Soul, not doing this or that, but wholly, incessantly given up to God, to be where and what, and how he pleases. (Law, *The Works of the Reverend William Law*, 9:183)

1.   Invite the group to share special prayer concerns. They may want to refer to the Reflecting and Recording time in Day 1, or to Day 2 when they named persons who were bearing crosses or the causes of sorrow and tears in their own life, or when they thought about persons who were mourning. After each concern, ask a volunteer to offer a brief prayer.

2.   Invite those who are willing to offer brief prayers on behalf of persons who have shared special needs in this session.

3.   *Leader,* close by praying the following prayer:

Dear Jesus,
    Be present in us in a powerful way today and in the coming days. Possess our minds, our hearts, our wills.
    Let no word cross our lips that is not your word.
    Let no thoughts be cultivated that are not your thoughts.
    Let no deeds be done that are not an expression of your love and concern.
    May your presence be so real in us that others will no longer see us but you, Lord Jesus.
    May we be cheered by your presence and move through these coming days with no hint of anxiety so that your peace may flow from our lives. Amen.

Offer a two- or three-sentence benediction.

Week Four

Blessed Are the Meek

DAY 1

A Study in Contrasts

Yet a little while, and the wicked will be no more;
though you look diligently for their place,
    they will not be there.
But the meek shall inherit the land,
    and delight themselves in abundant prosperity.

The wicked plot against the righteous,
    and gnash their teeth at them;
but the LORD laughs at the wicked, for he sees that their day is coming.

The wicked draw the sword and bend their bows
    to bring down the poor and needy,
    to kill those who walk uprightly;
their sword shall enter their own heart,
    and their bows shall be broken.

Better is a little that the righteous person has
    than the abundance of many wicked.
For the arms of the wicked shall be broken,
    but the LORD upholds the righteous. (Psalm 37:10-17)

For decades a certain man strutted in the power of a tyrant. In May 2002, Mark Bowden described him in *The Atlantic Monthly*:

His titles are many: the Anointed One, Glorious Leader, Direct Descendant of the Prophet, President of Iraq, Chairman of its Revolutionary Command Council, field marshal of its armies, doctor of its laws, and Great Uncle to all its people. Giant statues depicting him and larger-than-life portraits adorn all public places.

He rises daily at three in the morning, sleeping only four or five hours a night; rarely if ever in the same bed twice. Because of a slipped disk, he swims vigorously every morning and still walks with a slight limp. Because of that, it is strictly forbidden to film him walking. To approach him unsolicited in public is to be beaten within an inch of your life.

Shipments of fresh food are flown in twice a week from around the world—lobster, shrimp, fish, lots of lean meat. They come first to his nuclear scientists, who x-ray them and test them for radiation and poison. Then the food is transported under armed guard to his twenty palaces; there three elaborate meals a day are prepared by European-trained chefs under the scrutiny of armed guards. Where he will eat on a given day, no one knows. Everyone is ready.

His chief model of governance: Joseph Stalin. His way of ruling is pure terror: treacherous, tyrannical cruelty. He ascended to power in 1979. He summoned the entire Revolutionary Command Council and hundreds of other party leaders to a conference hall in Baghdad. Wearing his military uniform, he strode to the lectern and stood behind two microphones, waving a large cigar. He announced that there had been a betrayal—a Syrian plot. There were traitors among them, and he proceeded to have the names of all the conspirators read as one by one armed guards escorted them out—sixty of them. It was a farce. After secret trials they were led to the firing squad where their mouths were taped shut to squelch any troublesome last words. . . .

He has had two of his sons-in-law executed for perceived disloyalty. (Adapted from Bowden, "Tales of the Tyrant," *The Atlantic Monthly* 289 [May 2002]: 35)

Saddam Hussein is his name, and his singular aim was to rule the world. We think of him as the most recent dramatic demonstration of perceived power and might against which Jesus' word thunders as a mind-throbbing contradiction: "Blessed are the meek, for they will inherit the earth."

For over two decades, Hussein "inherited"—in other words, controlled—a huge piece of the earth . . . an entire nation. Let us be quick to acknowledge that how Hussein was "disinherited"—by war—is a demonstration of power that this third Beatitude of Jesus challenges as well. It is the picture of the power, the control, the tyranny, the military might that causes our minds to stand at attention when we read "Blessed are the meek." From pharaohs to Philistines and from Nebuchadnezzar to Herod in the Bible, from Bloody Mary to Adolf Hitler and from Stalin to Hussein in secular history, tyrants are not new, and those who would scorn the notion of meekness and defy any hint of it in their lifestyle are plentiful. In every century since Jesus, a plethora of witnesses rises up to challenge his absurd contention: "Blessed are the meek."

In a sermon titled "Tyrants, Terrorists, and the Meekness of God," John David Walt, Dean of the Chapel at Asbury Seminary, provides a panoramic biblical picture of the nature of meekness which Jesus said was blessed:

> Meekness—it conjures up images of an old woman (Sarah) counting the stars and daring to believe she was counting her descendants when she had not one.
>
> Meekness—it looks like a tiny baby (Moses) placed by parents in an ark of reeds—civil disobedience—and gently navigated right into the palace of the pharaoh.
>
> Meekness—it looks like the young widow Ruth, clinging to Naomi on the road to Bethlehem, becoming the one through whom Naomi's name and lineage would be preserved, preparing the humble origins of King David.
>
> Meekness—it reminds us of the unlikely Gideon, threshing wheat in a winepress, hiding from the enemy and called to be a deliverer. And with an army pared down from thirty thousand to three hundred, armed with trumpets, torches, and clay pots, Gideon proved victorious. . . .
>
> Meekness—it looks like the anointed, unknown boy king, shedding the armor of Saul like ill-fitting clothes, taking up five smooth stones, facing the giant, and saying, "You come against me with sword and spear and javelin, but I come against you in the name of the Lord Almighty, the God of the armies of Israel, whom you have defied" (1 Sam. 17:45, NIV).
>
> Meekness—it looks like the boy Samuel hearing the Lord calling his name in the middle of the night and making his answer: "Speak, for your servant is listening" (1 Sam. 3:10, NIV).

In the midst of a world that greedily thirsts for power comes our meek God. Born in the small town of Bethlehem (which means "the house of bread"), in a stable no less. Cradled in a feeding trough. The image of the invisible God, the one in whom the Word of God dwelt in fullness—bodily. Wrapped in swaddling cloths, enthroned on a mattress of hay. Our God is an awesome God! Our God is also a meek God, who comes in the person of Jesus to make a heart-stopping, mind-boggling pronouncement: "Blessed are the meek."

Reflecting and Recording

Without long thought, list six words to describe Saddam Hussein:

1.

2.

3.

4.

5.

6.

Now consider Jesus. Beside as many of the words listed above as possible, write the word's opposite if you think it describes Jesus.

Spend a bit of time pondering this question: What persons do I know in influential and powerful positions that I consider meek?

During the Day

See how many persons you can identify who have a mark of meekness about them, as you understand the word.

DAY 2

The Song of Moses and the Song of the Lamb

Then I saw another portent in heaven, great and amazing: seven angels with seven plagues, which are the last, for with them the wrath of God is ended. And I saw what appeared to be a sea of glass mixed with fire, and those who had conquered the beast and its image and the number of its name, standing beside the sea of glass with harps of God in their hands. And they sang the song of Moses, the servant of God, and the song of the Lamb:
"Great and amazing are your deeds,
      Lord God the Almighty!
Just and true are your ways,
      King of the nations!
Lord, who will not fear
      and glorify your name?
For you alone are holy.
All nations will come and worship before you,
      for your judgments have been revealed." (Rev. 15:1-4)

The biblical "poster persons" for meekness are Moses and Jesus. The description of Moses boldly claims, "Now the man Moses was very meek, above all the men which were upon the face of the earth" (Num. 12:3, KJV). But this claim could no longer be made after Jesus, the incarnation of meekness, for none can compare to him. Of all that could be said of Jesus, his own self-identification is the ultimate description: "I am meek and lowly in heart" (Matt. 11:29, KJV).

The pattern of meekness personified by Moses in the Old Testament and the incarnation of God in Christ as "meek and lowly" are sublimely brought together in John's revelation of worship in heaven. Those who have gone through the tribulation and "conquered the beast" were rejoicing ". . . with harps of God in their hands . . . they sang the song of Moses, the servant of God, and the song of the Lamb" (Rev. 15:2-3). Look at the two: Moses and the Lamb, two pictures of meekness.

Moses' mom and dad had to say good-bye to their baby because Pharaoh was killing all the male Hebrew children. They put him in a little boat of reeds and floated him out into the Nile River, expecting God to deliver. Blessed are the meek, for they trust in and depend on God. The future deliverer of his people was a helpless baby in a boat, "up the river without a paddle."

Rescued by Pharaoh's daughter, Moses grew up as a prince in Pharaoh's court—nothing "meek" there. He witnessed the cruel and tyrannical injustices against his people. Unawares, as is often the case, a revolutionary anger boiled within. It exploded one day when he came upon an Egyptian task master lashing a downtrodden Hebrew. That was the breaking point. Soon the sand was red with the blood of the Egyptian slain by Moses. Conscience-stricken and afraid he would be found out, Moses fled Pharaoh's court and ended up on the back side of Midian—a fugitive sheepherder in exile, "an alien in a foreign land" (Exod. 2:22, NIV).

Here is a clear antidote to the thinking that meekness is an inherited quality or a matter of temperament. This account completely destroys the image of a meek person as somewhat sparkless and spineless—quiet, placid, easygoing. Does the life of Moses thus far confirm any of the traditional notions we have about meekness? Moses as a young man had boiling blood that issued in murder—but something happened to him and he became the person described as "the meekest on earth"! It was those wilderness years, tending sheep, that transformed Moses' anger into the seasoned stuff of meekness. John David Walt says:

> For all of his upbringing and credentials, finally [Moses] was fit for use in the hands of Yahweh. And through his meekness came a demonstration of the supernatural power of God. The baby who was drawn up out of the water would humbly raise the staff of God and part the sea. (Walt, "Tyrants, Terrorists, and the Meekness of God," sermon, September 5, 2002)

At the heart of God's expression of meekness we find meek leaders—Moses chief among them. He learned to curb the powerful passions that, in his early life, had controlled him. Notice this: he did not extinguish the flaming passion that caused him to kill the Egyptian; he chained it, harnessed it in a way that stripped it of its savagery, and transformed it into the service of almighty God.

Meekness does not mean being without passion, commitment, and driving power. To the end of his days, Moses had that passion—a passion that caused Aaron and the idolaters who had made the golden calf to tremble when Moses, expressing his holy wrath, broke the two commandment tablets into pieces at the foot of Mount Sinai.

That's Moses the servant—but what about the Lamb, Jesus, who extends the invitation, "Come unto me, all you who are weary and burdened, and I will give you rest. Take my yoke upon you and learn from me, for I am gentle [meek] and humble in heart, and you shall find rest for your souls" (Matt. 11:28-29, NIV)?

Again we see the passionate quality of meekness: Jesus in his righteous indignation holds a whip made from cords and overturns the tables of the money changers and the benches of those selling doves. All of our stereotypical thoughts about meekness are shattered when we look at Jesus and see in him not signs of cowardly weakness but of splendid strength. His refusal to be infuriated under rebuke does not signal a lack of spirit. When he was reviled, he did not revile in return; this is a sign of strength, not weakness. F. W. Boreham expresses it well:

> The light of heaven is on his face, but the fires of hell burn in his breast; God alone knows the awful struggle proceeding within. Would it be strength to yield to his baser self, to utter the word that trembles on his tongue, to strike the blow for which his fist is automatically clenched? Or is it strength to hold the fiendish passions under, to return a smile for a frown, a blessing for a curse? (Boreham, *The Heavenly Octave*, 45)

So many connections—the song of Moses and the song of the Lamb. In the story of Jesus, the baby is not in a reed basket floating on the Nile but in a rough feeding trough surrounded by animals behind a public inn. And he's not just another baby; this time he's the Son of God. In Jesus, the assault will not be against those who oppress God's people but on the ultimate tyrants of sin and death.

Like Moses, Jesus passes through a time of preparation. At age thirty, summoned by the Spirit of God, he is driven into the desert to confront the seductive powers of darkness. He has only one instrument to guide him—the Word of God. That Word has taken root in his heart, and it shapes his ministry. The third Beatitude is an expression of that Word:

> Yet a little while and the wicked will be no more;
>   though you look diligently for their place, they will not be there.
> But the meek shall inherit the land,
>   and delight themselves in abundant prosperity. (Ps. 37:10-11)

Reflecting and Recording

Accepting Moses and Jesus as outstanding expressions of meekness, whom do you know that you would describe as meek? Name and describe that person here. What qualities of this person cause you to think of him or her as meek?

Would the person you named and described be considered meek by popular understanding of the word? Would you have thought of that person as meek before your consideration of Moses and Jesus? Spend a few minutes thinking about meekness—how you have thought about it in the past, how we popularly think of it.

■ ■ ■

During the Day

Seek to engage a person in a discussion about meekness—what it means to be meek and what he or she thinks about Jesus' word "Blessed are the meek."

✠

DAY 3

Brought under Control

William Barclay called *meekness* "the most untranslatable of words." I think the word *meek* has been misunderstood and devalued through the centuries. According to the Online Etymology Dictionary (www.etymonline.com), in the Middle Ages the word meant "gentle; courteous; kind." Now it means "easily imposed on; submissive." Certainly the earlier meaning is a much better translation of the Greek word for *meek*. The latter definition, carrying suggestions of weakness, colorlessness, and lack of passion, most certainly does not resemble the definition of the word as it is used in scripture. In scripture, one finds nothing weak or timidly submissive about true meekness.

On Day 1, we considered a description of Saddam Hussein at the height of his "glory," seeing himself as the "Anointed One," the "Glorious Leader." Nine months after Iraq was invaded by the United States and Britain, Saddam was captured (December 13, 2003). He was hiding in a six-by-eight-foot hole in the ground near a farmhouse. He was ragged, dirty, unkempt, shabby, with long hair and beard. Newscasters described him as looking like a homeless person or a rat in a hole. Newsman Tom Brokaw reflected on the giant statues and larger-than-life portraits that a few months earlier had pervaded the public places and buildings of Iraq, but now Saddam lived in a "meek and utterly degraded way."

That is a telling misunderstanding of meekness: a once-powerful ruler, living in opulent luxury, reduced to hiding like a rat in a hole.

We learned, as we considered the models of Moses and Jesus, that meekness is certainly not weakness and cowering defeat. Scripture contains other wonderful demonstrations of this fact. King David, on one occasion, was cursed by a man from the clan of Saul, the former king. King David was asked, "Why should this dead dog curse my lord the king? Let me go over and take off his head." But the king would not allow it. Instead, he humbly took the cursing, saying, "It may be that the LORD will look on my distress, and the LORD will repay me with good for this cursing of me today" (2 Sam. 16:5-14).

In the New Testament, Stephen demonstrates strength and passion. He speaks before the Sanhedrin, tracing the mighty acts of God, telling the stories of Abraham, Jacob, Moses, and David. He mounts his case for the cause of Christianity and then pronounces judgment:

> You stiff-necked people, uncircumcised in heart and ears, you are forever opposing the Holy Spirit, just as your ancestors used to do. Which of the prophets did your ancestors not persecute? They killed those who foretold the coming of the Righteous One, and now you have become his betrayers and murderers. You are the ones that received the law as ordained by angels, and yet you have not kept it. (Acts 7:51-53)

When the people heard these things, they were furious, and they dragged Stephen out of the city and began to stone him. While they were stoning him, Stephen prayed, "Lord Jesus, receive my spirit" (Acts 7:59). Then he fell on his knees and cried out, "Lord, do not hold this sin against them" (v. 60).

Nothing weak and colorless here—either in David or in Stephen.

The meek are constrained, not by self-discipline alone but primarily by God's love. They use their indignation—even their anger—not on behalf of themselves but on behalf of others.

One of the Greek words for meekness, *praus*, can be translated "domesticated." This word describes a wild animal that has been broken, brought under control. The animal has now been trained. It has learned to respond to reins and follow commands. If we haven't seen this process in person, we've seen it in many movies—a wild horse that has been broken and trained, responding to the direction of its master.

That image provides a good picture of this untranslatable word, *meekness*. A meek person is not weak but God-controlled. She is free because she is under the control of God. She has prayed the following prayer and lives by it:

Make me a captive, Lord, and then I shall be free.
Force me to render up my sword, and I shall conqueror be.
I sink in life's alarms when by myself I stand;
imprison me within thine arms, and strong shall be my hand.

My heart is weak and poor until it master find;
it has no spring of action sure, it varies with the wind.
It cannot freely move till thou hast wrought its chain;
Enslave it with thy matchless love, and deathless it shall reign.

(George Matheson, 1890, *The United Methodist Hymnal*, No. 421)

The picture is that of a person completely surrendered to Christ. Paul conveys that image when he speaks of himself as a prisoner of the Lord. That's quite a confession. Paul had a turbulent, unruly spirit until his Damascus road experience, when he came face-to-face with Christ, surrendered himself to Christ, and then was captured and guided by Christ's love.

Jesus says the meek shall inherit the earth. Why? Because the meek are open and flexible; they are free enough to receive what God has to give. The truth is that most of us are so filled with our own ideas that there's no room for other ideas. We're so certain of what is best for us and for the people we love that it's difficult for God to get through to us. We're so full of pride that we dart off in all directions, offering our alternative solutions. So, we're not able to accept what God offers. We don't have the meekness that produces a dynamic freedom open to God's graciousness. We don't have the meekness that demonstrates itself in abandonment to God as the potter of life—asking for God's guidance, God's shaping hand, to develop our life.

Reflecting and Recording

Do you know a person who would fit the definition of meekness as "domesticated"—like a wild horse, broken, brought under control? Name that person here:

Spend some time thinking about that person before and after he or she became meek. What made the difference? How did the change come about?

■ ■ ■

We made this statement above: "The meek are constrained, not by self-discipline alone but primarily by God's love." Spend some time thinking about what God's love adds to our effort at self-discipline.

■ ■ ■

Spend a few minutes thinking about how meekness makes us flexible in our thinking, attitudes, and how we relate to others.

■ ■ ■

During the Day

The "Make Me a Captive, Lord" prayer is printed on page 211. Cut it out, take it with you, and pray it often today and in the days ahead. Memorize it so that you can have it as a ready prayer.

✠

DAY 4

To Be Minded

One of the most beautiful descriptions of Jesus is not found in the Gospels but in this passage from Paul:

> who, though he was in the form of God,
>> did not regard equality with God
> as something to be exploited,
> but emptied himself,
>> taking the form of a slave,
>> being born in human likeness.
> And being found in human form,
>> he humbled himself
>> and became obedient to the point of death—
> even death on a cross. (Phil. 2:6-8)

Jesus' own words verify Paul's: "I am meek and lowly in heart" (Matt. 11:29, KJV).

These descriptions of Jesus provide a clue to the meaning of the third Beatitude: "Blessed are the meek, for they will inherit the earth." The Philippian passage from which the above verses are taken (2:5-11) begins, "Let each of you look not to your own interests, but to the interests of others. Let the same mind be in you that was in Christ Jesus . . ." (vv. 4-5). Some modern translations render it in such a way that the word *mind* is not used. For instance, the New International Version has it this way: "Your attitude should be the same as that of Christ Jesus" (v. 5). *The Message* renders it thus: "Think of yourselves the way Christ Jesus thought of himself." While these translations may help us in understanding and expression, they do not plumb the depth of what Paul is talking about when he describes Jesus. He employs the same Greek verb that occurs in Mark 8, where Jesus tells Peter he does not think as God thinks. In that setting, Peter was very bold, even arrogant, and began to rebuke Jesus because Jesus had spoken about being rejected, about being killed, and about rising from the dead. In response, Jesus said to Peter, "Get behind me, Satan! For you are setting your mind not on divine things but on human things" (Mark 8:33).

The Greek word is *phroneite*, which literally means "to be minded." So, in this Philippian passage, Paul is calling us to "be minded" as Christ is minded.

Meekness, then, relates to character. It is a disposition of mind that grows out of who a person is. It is not a matter of temperament or an inherited personality trait. Meekness is learned and practiced until it becomes part of our identity. It is an attribute of *being*, not *doing*. There is a real sense in which we can't live the new life this and the other Beatitudes describe apart from the new birth Jesus provides.

The grace of Jesus, making us new creatures in Christ, transforms and empowers us to receive the blessings of being poor in spirit, mourning, and being meek. As is true of those who are poor in spirit, those who mourn do so because of their awareness of the depth of their inadequacy and need. The same truth applies to the meek. Take the whole matter of forgiveness. If we never feel the need to be forgiven, we will never know the full richness, wonder, and joy of that simple word—*forgiveness*. Supporting this truth, J. Randall Nichols wrote of an experience while visiting the Greek island of Corfu:

> Some of the most beautiful music I ever heard was the chanting of Greek peasant women, tears streaming down their lined and hardened faces, in a church on Corfu on Good Friday. I asked someone why they were weeping. "Because," he said, "their Christ is dead." I have often thought that I will never understand what resurrection means until I can weep like that. (Nichols, quoted in George and McGrath, eds., *For All the Saints*, 23)

> Nichols's point is that we can never appreciate the joy and hope of the resurrection, unless we have been plunged into the sense of hopelessness and helplessness which pervaded that first Good Friday. What is true of the resurrection is also true of forgiveness. Christian spirituality is grounded in an awareness of being a condemned sinner—an experience that is utterly transformed by divine forgiveness. We can never understand what forgiveness really means until we have wept the tears of condemnation. (George and McGrath, eds., *For All the Saints*, 23)

This is not a once-and-for-all "done deal." We live with these Beatitudes and become aware of our pride and selfishness, our divided minds, our hungering and thirsting for bread that does not satisfy, our stony rather than tender and merciful hearts, and we are driven to our knees in shame and contrition. Through our tears of repentance, we see the cross and we hear our crucified Lord pronounce, "Blessed! Blessed! Blessed!"

Reflecting and Recording

Spend a few minutes reflecting on this claim: Meekness relates to character; it is learned and practiced until it becomes part of our identity.

■ ■ ■

In the designated columns, write a word or short phrase describing what meekness is and isn't.

Meekness is	Meekness isn't

How does your description of what meekness is and isn't confirm or question the statement "Meekness is an attribute of *being*, not *doing*"?

■ ■ ■

During the Day

Pray often, and seek to memorize the "Make Me a Captive, Lord" prayer.

✠

DAY 5

Look Not to Your Own Interests

If then there is any encouragement in Christ, any consolation from love, any sharing in the Spirit, any compassion and sympathy, make my joy complete: be of the same mind, having the same love, being in full accord and of one mind. Do nothing from selfish ambition or conceit, but in humility regard others as better than yourselves. Let each of you look not to your own interests, but to the interests of others. (Phil. 2:1-4)

Division existed within the church at Philippi, unresolved tension that brought reproach to the cause of Christ. In light of that situation, Paul had a crucial message for the Philippians: That conflict could be resolved—but only if the Philippians experienced a change of heart. The basic problem of the Christians at Philippi was they had different "minds." Each was thinking his or her own way. If the divisions were to be healed, minds had to be transformed, and Paul described the result of that transformation: "Do nothing from selfish ambition or conceit, but in humility regard others as better than yourselves. Let each of you look not to your own interests, but to the interests of others" (Phil. 2:3-4).

Selfish ambition—isn't this the sin that most contradicts meekness? Sin distorts our orientation, making us self-oriented. The redemption offered by Jesus Christ undoes our distorted orientation—instead of turning inward and being interested only in ourselves, we become concerned about others and compassionate toward them.

We often wonder, *What's in it for me?* But that question is not a part of the mind of Christ, so it should not motivate the Christian. Can you find any instance in scripture where self-interest was Jesus' first consideration? Jesus gave great clarity to the Old Testament call of God, "Love your neighbor as yourself" (Lev. 19:18). He expressed meekness as a lifestyle, saying: "Love one another as I have loved you. No one has greater love than this, to lay down one's life for one's friends" (John 15:12-13). By presenting himself as the shepherd who willingly sacrificed himself for his sheep, Jesus changed the pattern of personal priorities.

"Blessed are the meek," Jesus said, "for they will inherit the earth." At the very least, this Beatitude exhorts us, "Look not to your own interests." You can't be meek, as Jesus calls us to be, and be concerned about how you appear to others. You can't be meek and spend your life preoccupied with your own status. Though dogmatic and hard to accept, this statement is true: When we live in the kingdom of self, we shut ourselves out of the kingdom of heaven.

"Blessed are the meek, for they will inherit the earth." They need not worry about their own interests, but because of their meekness, having the mind of Christ, they will be blessed beyond their imagining.

Eugene H. Peterson paraphrases Philippians 2:1-4 like this:

If you've gotten anything at all out of following Christ, if his love has made any difference in your life, if being in a community of the Spirit means anything to you, if you have a heart, if you *care*—then do me a favor: Agree with each other, love each other, be deep-spirited friends. Don't push your way to the front; don't sweet-talk your way to the top. Put yourself aside, and help others get ahead. Don't be obsessed with getting your own advantage. Forget yourselves long enough to lend a helping hand. (*The Message*)

Reflecting and Recording

In the space provided beside Philippians 2:1-4 at the beginning of today's reading, write those verses in your own words.

In what ways have you failed to respond to the Christian call "Look not to your own interests"? Write a brief prayer of confession, asking God to help you "love your neighbor as yourself."

During the Day

If any persons you named in your Reflecting and Recording of Days 2 and 3 are living, call or write them, thanking them for their model and witness.

Continue praying and memorizing the "Make Me a Captive, Lord" prayer, using the affirmation card.

✠

DAY 6

A Metaphor for Meekness

[Jesus said], "The hour has come for the Son of Man to be glorified. Very truly, I tell you, unless a grain of wheat falls into the earth and dies, it remains just a single grain; but if it dies, it bears much fruit. Those who love their life lose it, and those who hate their life in this world will keep it for eternal life. Whoever serves me must follow me, and where I am, there will my servant be also. Whoever serves me, the Father will honor." (John 12:23-26)

John's Gospel gives a rather dramatic metaphor for a central core of the good news: "Unless a grain of wheat falls into the earth and dies, it remains just a single grain; but if it dies, it bears much fruit" (John 12:24).

One of the Christians we have admired most through the years—and whose friendship we have treasured—is Dr. Donald English. He was a marvelous preacher and an outstanding New Testament scholar. It was a great joy to work with him in the World Methodist Council and in World Methodist Evangelism. We especially remember one of his sermons. He penetrated our minds and hearts by inviting us to imagine that we were a bunch of tulip bulbs, comfortably tucked away in a wooden box on the garden store shelf. Safe, dry, warm—very comfortable. One day a huge hand reaches down into the box and pulls out a handful of bulbs. The bulbs that are left behind say, "Whew! That was a close call! How fortunate that we were left behind! We have heard what will happen to those bulbs. The gardener will dig a hole in the ground and bury them in it. They will die down there, and the earth will freeze over them. We're the fortunate ones! We're still safe and secure in our cozy little box."

In his inimitable way of preaching, Donald reminded us that spring would come; the snow would melt; moisture would penetrate the earth. Then the miracle of nature would happen: those bulbs that had been buried in the ground would spring forth in a spectacular expression of beauty—"tulipness"—that the other bulbs, safely tucked away in that box back in the garden store, would never comprehend.

An ongoing awareness of the transitoriness of human life, which is not normally present in most of us, is an essential aspect of meekness. J. I. Packer reminds us of the importance of the Puritan understanding of life as "a gymnasium and dressing room where we are all prepared for heaven." Packer insists that a "readiness to die" is "the first step in learning to live." (Packer, *A Quest for Godliness*, 13)

As we reckon with death, we appreciate each new day of life. C. S. Lewis put it succinctly: "Nothing that has not died will be resurrected." (Lewis, "Membership," in *The Weight of Glory and Other Addresses*, 117)

Jesus was clear about it: "Those who love their life will lose it, and those who hate their life in this world will keep it for eternal life" (John 12:25). We may think that to be an exaggeration—hating life versus loving life—but the point is clear: If we try to pridefully hold on to life, protect it, possess it, and hold it selfishly unto ourselves, we will lose it. Our life won't have any meaning, and it certainly will not issue in joy.

This metaphor of the seed dying in the earth, germinating to be reborn to new life, is connected with all the Beatitudes but especially with Jesus' pronouncement of blessedness on the meek. Modern wisdom might suggest: "How blessed are the powerful. How blessed are the self-sufficient. How blessed are the proud and the strong, for they shall control the earth." But Jesus said *no*. The meek, the gentle—those willing to serve—will be blessed and will "inherit the earth."

In this third Beatitude, Jesus underscores one of the qualities of his own life, and he calls us to claim and cultivate it for ourselves. There is a sense in which the meaning of this Beatitude is discovered in the promise of Jesus: "Take my yoke upon you, and learn of me, for I am meek and lowly in heart: and ye shall find rest unto your souls. For my yoke is easy, and my burden is light" (Matt. 11:29-30, KJV).

The life of Jesus, the incarnate Son of God, reveals the meaning of meekness. Obedience was the essence of his life. Not only in Gethsemane, though it reached a pinnacle of commitment there, but throughout Jesus' life, his constant prayer was, "Not my will, but thine, be done" (Luke 22:42, RSV).

Reflecting and Recording

Spend a few minutes reflecting on this claim: Pride is our declaration of freedom from God; meekness is the stance/style of those who know they are completely dependent on God.

■ ■ ■

Think about a time when your life most resembled a seed buried in the ground, having to die (germinate) in order to live. Describe that experience here.

Recall a time when you responded to Jesus' offer, "Take my yoke upon you, and learn from me; for I am gentle and humble in heart, and you will find rest for your souls." Live for a while in the memory of that time.

■ ■ ■

How alive is that experience now? In what way are you "wearing Jesus' yoke"?

■ ■ ■

During the Day

Seek to engage someone in conversation about the "yoke of Christ" and a seed buried in the ground as metaphors for meekness.

DAY 7

Inherit the Earth

Do not deceive yourselves. If you think that you are wise in this age, you should become fools so that you may become wise. For the wisdom of this world is foolishness with God. For it is written,

"He catches the wise in their craftiness,"

and again,

"The Lord knows the thoughts of the wise, that they are futile."

So let no one boast about human leaders. For all things are yours, whether Paul or Apollos or Cephas or the world or life or death or the present or the future—all belong to you, and you belong to Christ, and Christ belongs to God. (1 Cor. 3:18-23)

What is Jesus talking about? "Blessed are the meek, for they will *inherit the earth*" (emphasis ours). Clearly he is not talking about earthly territory but about a quality of life on earth. All that Christ accomplished through his life, death, and resurrection is our inheritance. This was the witness of Paul: "All things are yours."

In Romans 8, Paul mentions that we are "heirs of God and joint heirs with Christ." Our inheritance—inheriting the earth—means Christ will supply all of our needs. But the inheritance belongs to the meek.

This is where Adam and Eve missed the mark; they were not meek but proud. God had told them they could enjoy the abundance of the Garden of Eden with one exception: they were not to eat of the tree of the knowledge of good and evil (Gen. 2:17). Their lives would be bountiful, beautiful, and blessed—if they were faithful.

Adam and Eve's story provides clear witness that pride is the root of original sin. They wanted to know everything. They were presumptuous enough to think that God didn't really mean what he said. With a little enticement, they went to the tree of knowledge and ate its forbidden fruit. They ignored the one request God had made of them. Their pride deceived them into the sin of disobedience.

Their sin is our sin: the need to be "in charge," to control our own destiny. In our pride, we declare our independence from God. To want to be like God is right and good within itself. This is how God made us—in the divine image. The problem is that we want to be like God without surrendering our autonomy. Controlled by our self-will, we want a life of godlike existence independent of God. Only when we give up our self-centered attempt to run our own lives—when we decide to live in total dependence upon God—do we become joint heirs with Christ and inherit the earth. Forgiveness and redemption form a part of that inheritance. Living a Christ-filled life, by the power of the Holy Spirit, is the ongoing inheritance.

Our inheritance is not a one-time gift; it is residual and ongoing. It is not only what Christ did but also what he will do. At the right time and in the right way our needs will be met. So, when we are meek, we can wait for each new payment on our inheritance.

To be meek is to depend on God. Jesus promised that if we trust in him, we will inherit the kingdom that he has prepared for us (Matt. 25:34). The gift that is ours, the inheritance of the meek, is eternal life (Matt. 19:29). Paul speaks of the "glorious inheritance among the saints" (Eph. 1:18), and Peter reminds us that in Christ we have "an inheritance that can never perish, spoil or fade—kept in heaven for you" (1 Pet. 1:4, NIV). But that inheritance is ours in an ongoing kind of way as we "who through faith are shielded by God's power until the coming of the salvation that is ready to be revealed in the last time" (v. 5).

Our inheritance is the inexhaustible power of the Holy Spirit, sufficient for every situation. It is wisdom, knowledge, discernment, insight, guidance—what we need when we need it. Life may be unpredictable, but our inheritance—the presence of Christ through the Holy Spirit—is predictable. To know that we serve a loving God who has come to us as a saving Christ and provides for us now the empowering Holy Spirit—this is the inheritance of the meek.

Reflecting and Recording

Spend a few minutes pondering the following thoughts:

If we admit our inadequacy, we can have God's adequacy.

■ ■ ■

The key to Christian sufficiency is realizing that everything comes from God and nothing comes from us. Life may be unpredictable, but the inheritance that is ours—the presence of Christ through the Holy Spirit—is predictable.

■ ■ ■

Consider your congregation. How does it go about doing its work and establishing priorities? To what degree is the following statement true: "The greatest problem in the church is trying to do God's work with human strength"?

■ ■ ■

If you are a part of a group sharing this workbook, you will be meeting sometime today. Look back over the content of this week, your Reflecting and Recording, and make notes about ideas you want to discuss and questions you want to ask.

Spend the remaining time praying for persons in your group. If you are not in a group, write a brief prayer claiming your inheritance, surrendering your will to Christ, and asking him to make you meek.

During the Day

At various times during the day, reflect on this statement: "Everything comes from God; nothing comes from me." Continue praying the words of "Make Me a Captive, Lord."

✠

Group Meeting
for Week Four

Leader: You will need a dry-erase board or newsprint for this session.

Paul advised the Philippians, "Let your conversation be as it becometh the gospel of Christ" (Phil. 1:27, KJV). Most other translations do not use the word *conversation;* rather, they use phrases like "Live your life in a manner worthy of the gospel" (Col. 4:6). Our conversation—our speech—indicates the content of our life. Thus, Paul urged the Colossians, "Let your speech always be gracious, seasoned with salt," and he admonished the Ephesians, "Let no evil talk come out of your mouths, but only what is useful for building up, . . . so that your words may give grace to those who hear" (4:29). Most of us may not have experienced the dynamic potential of the conversation to which Paul calls the Philippians. Life is found in communion with God and in conversation with others.

Speaking and listening with this sort of deep meaning is challenging. All of us have experiences that we cannot easily talk about. Genuinely listening to others and reflecting back what you heard them say can help them think clearly and gain perspective. Listening, then, is an act of love. When we listen to someone, we say nonverbally: "I value you. You are important." When we listen in a way that makes a difference, we surrender ourselves to the other person, saying, "I will hear what you have to say and will receive you as I receive your words." When we speak in a way that makes a difference, we speak for the sake of others; thus we contribute to their understanding and wholeness.

Sharing Together

1. Ask if anyone would like to share something special that has happened during the past week or two, connected with using this workbook.

2. Spend a few minutes talking about how group members are using the During the Day suggestions and what difference it is making in their lives.

3. Spend six to eight minutes discussing how your understanding of meekness may have changed as a result of considering Moses and Jesus as the biblical "poster persons" for meekness.

4. Invite two or three persons to name and describe a meek person they know.

5. Invite the group to reflect on the descriptions that have been shared and to list on a chart in single words or phrases what it means to be meek.

6. Invite someone to read the last paragraph of the commentary for Day 3 (paragraph preceding Reflecting and Recording). Then discuss the meaning of meekness as being "under the control of God," "abandonment to God," "free enough to receive what God has to give," "constrained not by self-discipline alone but primarily by God's love."

7. Write on the board or newsprint words or phrases group members give you to complete this sentence: "Meekness is . . ." Then write their completion of the sentence "Meekness is not . . ."

8. Spend eight to ten minutes discussing the statement, "Meekness is *being* something, not *doing* something" and "to be minded" as the literal meaning of Paul's call to "let the same mind be in you that was in Christ Jesus."

9. On Day 6 we considered the idea that the seed buried in the ground must germinate (die) in order to live. Invite two or three persons to share the experience they recorded on Day 6 of the occasion when they came nearest to owning this as a metaphor for their life.

10. Invite one or two persons to share any experience when they intentionally responded to Jesus' call, "Take my yoke upon you, and learn of me: for I am meek and lowly in heart: and ye shall find rest unto your souls" (Matt. 11:29, KJV).

11. Invite persons who wish to share any new or especially challenging insight they have received about pride and meekness in their use of the workbook this week.

12. Spend whatever time you have left discussing the assertion, "*Pride* is our declaration of freedom from God; *meekness* is the stance/style of those who know they are completely dependent on God."

Praying Together

1.   If anyone knows the tune to the hymn "Make Me a Captive, Lord," lead the group in singing the verses printed on page 98.

2.   Corporate prayer is one of the great blessings of Christian community. We invite you to go deeper now, experimenting with the possibilities of corporate prayer by sharing in the fashion described here:
   - Bow in silence and in prayerful concern. The leader calls the name of a person in the group, and someone else in the group offers a brief prayer for the individual named.
   - The leader calls another name, and that person is prayed for.
   - The prayers may be brief—two or three sentences—or longer. Think of the person whose name is called. What concern or need has been shared tonight or in the past weeks that could be mentioned in prayer? You may want to express gratitude for the person's life and witness, the role he or she plays in the group, or that person's ministry in the community. Someone may be seeking direction or may need to make a crucial decision. Let someone pray for each individual in a particular way.

3.   Close your time by praying together the Lord's Prayer. As you pray this prayer, remember that the prayer links you with Christians of all times and places in universal praise, confession, thanksgiving, and intercession.

Week Five

Righteousness and Mercy

✠

DAY 1

Basic Human Yearnings

Blessed are those who hunger and thirst for righteousness, for they will be filled. Blessed are the merciful, for they will receive mercy. (Matthew 5:6-7)

This week we turn to righteousness and mercy, two intimately connected aspects of God's character. Righteousness and mercy go together because justice is part of God's righteousness. Mercy is needed for justice to truly be justice; without it, justice slides dangerously toward revenge. Mercy, on the other hand, is in danger of becoming *denial*—or in the language of recovery, *enabling*—without an honest recognition of the wrong that has been committed and the need for repentance, restitution, and appropriate consequences. We focus first on righteousness.

Righteousness may very well be the keynote of Jesus' entire Sermon on the Mount. The eighth and ninth Beatitudes pronounce blessing on the persecuted. They address not just any persecution, but persecution for *righteousness'* sake.

We better understand Jesus' words about righteousness when we hear and examine them in relation to the prevailing standards of righteousness in his day. Two things characterized those standards. One, they were external. People kept the rules and regulations because they were expected to, not because they believed them. In his inimitable way, Clarence Jordan, a New Testament Greek scholar who gave us the Cotton Patch version of the New Testament, described their righteousness as "something like perfume—it wasn't a part of you but if you had it on, it made you smell real sweet." Rather snidely, Jordan added, "Of course, everybody recognized the odor, but that didn't matter, because they used it, too." (Jordan, *Sermon on the Mount*, 28)

Jesus addressed this distorted understanding of righteousness, elaborating on this Beatitude in a section of his Sermon on the Mount (Matt. 6:1-18). He began, "Beware of practicing your piety before others in order to be seen by them; for then you have no reward from your Father in heaven" (6:1). On and on he went, addressing the issues of giving money, praying, and fasting, which lie at the heart of religion and righteousness. None of these is to be practiced for others to see. Nor are we to expect recognition and praise from others for what we do. "So whenever you give alms, do not sound a trumpet before you, as the hypocrites do in the synagogues and in the streets, so that they may be praised by others. Truly I tell you, they have received their reward" (v. 2).

The motive for righteousness was reward. This was the second characteristic. According to Clarence Jordan:

> Primarily the reward desired was the praise of man. To be well thought of was more highly desired than to be rich. In order to get and hold public approval, a man would sacrifice his own integrity, or perhaps his own son, or his best friend, or even his God. Incredible as it seems, men would even pretend they were serving God in order to please man. (Jordan, *Sermon on the Mount*, 28–29)

The thought of being righteous or serving God without reward was not a part of the Jewish thinking or experience. The elder brother in Jesus' parable of the prodigal son provides a good picture of it:

> "Listen! For all these years I have been working like a slave for you, and I have never disobeyed your command; yet you have never given me even a young goat so that I might celebrate with my friends. But when this son of yours came back, who has devoured your property with prostitutes, you killed the fatted calf for him!" Then the father said to him, "Son, you are always with me, and all that is mine is yours. But we had to celebrate and rejoice, because this brother of yours was dead and has come to life; he was lost and has been found." (Luke 15:29-32)

Before we respond with judgmental attitudes toward the Jewish people of Jesus' day, we need to examine our own religious practice. What about it is empty, external activity; how reward-oriented are we? We'll return to these questions, but now what righteousness is Jesus talking about?

Jesus says we will be blessed when we hunger and thirst for righteousness, but what exactly is that? Space does not permit an expansive discussion of righteousness, so it is important to emphasize that righteousness always mirrors God's will. When we hunger and thirst for righteousness, we desire that God's will be done in the world, and we place ourselves at God's disposal in order to make that happen. Hungering and thirsting for righteousness means that we yearn to have, be, and do whatever God wants—and we yearn for others the same. It means placing ourselves at the center of God's will for the world. It means striving for God's justice, God's rightness. It means desiring that our world will be in sync with what God wants for all of us.

This blessing is not for those who think about righteousness now and then or only when something external happens to bring it to their consciousness. Giving a gift basket at Christmas is not the same as paying a living wage or working diligently to end poverty. Attending a reconciliation service is not the same as inviting your neighbors, who belong to a different ethnic group, to dinner in order to get to know them better. Jesus' blessing is reserved for those who hunger and thirst for righteousness like a person who is starving for food or dying for water.

Reflecting and Recording

List some religious practices that form a regular, ongoing part of your life, such as worship attendance, Sunday school attendance, prayer, giving money, or reading scripture.

Put a check (✓) by those practices that are external. Circle those that are private, personal, and internal.

Spend some time examining the motives for your practices. Do you seek to impress others? Do you expect reward for what you do?

■ ■ ■

Write down the names of persons who come to mind in response to this question: Who are the most righteous persons I know?

Think about those persons. How well do they fit this description: desiring that God's will be done in the world and placing themselves at God's disposal in order to make it happen?

■ ■ ■

Spend some time reflecting on your own righteousness in light of the above understanding.

During the Day

Call or write as many of the persons you named as possible, affirming them by sharing why you called and why you thought of them as "righteous" persons.

DAY 2

The Starving Spirit

F. W. Boreham, who served as a pastor in New Zealand and Australia, was a powerful preacher. He titled his book on the Beatitudes *The Heavenly Octave*. Creative imagery is present throughout his book, with a special mind-grabbing image for the fourth Beatitude.

Boreham dreamed of approaching the City of Happiness, as it was known to the younger people, or the City of Blessedness, as older folks referred to it. As he walked around the city, he saw one gate at each corner and one in the center of each wall. Each gate was identified with a marble mosaic inscribed with precious stones. All the gates appeared the same size except one, the Western Gate, which was much wider and taller than any of the others. This gate also had the most traffic. In fact, so many people were waiting at the Western Gate that Boreham couldn't get close enough to make out the inscription.

Moving away from the Western Gate, he began to walk around the city wall. He discovered that over the first gate was written, "Blessed are the poor in spirit"; over the second, "Blessed are they that mourn." Other gates pronounced blessedness on the meek, the merciful, the pure in heart, the peacemakers, and those persecuted for righteousness. As he passed each gate, he noticed that few people were moving through these gates. He had traversed the city and found himself back where he had begun and saw again a great crowd approaching the Western Gate. He then realized one of the reasons for the congregation at that entrance:

> For I noticed that, from each of the other gates, a steady stream of people was turning sadly away. I saw thousands of pilgrims going from gate to gate, eager to enter the City of Blessedness, but finding no gate through which they were entitled to pass. They feared they were not sufficiently poor in spirit to enter the first; they had never sufficiently lamented their shortcomings and besetments to entitle them to enter the mourner's gate;

and they trembled when they thought how far they were from being meek. Then, passing the jostling crowd at the center gate, they looked at the *fifth*. "Alas!" they cried, "we are not merciful, although we dearly long to be!" And at the *sixth* they said: "We are not yet pure in heart; but oh, how we yearn after such snow-white purity!" And when they read the inscription over the *seventh* gate they said, "No, we are not peacemakers; but we should love to be!" And at the last—the Martyrs' Gate—they again turned away disconsolate. They had never dared the lions or the rack or the stake for their Saviour's sake: what right had they to enter there? And then it flashed upon me that the vast concourse at the great gate in the center of the Western wall was largely composed of these streams of disappointed people who had felt themselves disqualified for admission at the other gates. (Boreham, *The Heavenly Octave*, 54–55)

The keeper of the Martyrs' Gate ("Blessed are the persecuted") was not busy at all—little traffic there—and explained the reason for the vast numbers surging to the Western Gate, over which was the inscription, "Blessed are they that hunger and thirst after righteousness."

"You see," the keeper observed, "there are great numbers of people who turn sorrowfully away from these seven small gates. They go, for example, to the gate at the Southeast corner—the gate for the *Poor in Spirit*—and, when they read the inscription, they feel that they are not sufficiently lowly, and so they turn sadly away. Or they go to the gate on the North—the gate for the *Pure in Heart*—and they shrink from attempting to enter: they are too conscious of their own defilement. And so they begin to fancy that the City of Blessedness is not for them." . . .

"But," the keeper at the Martyrs' Gate continued, "it is one of the fundamental principles of the City of Blessedness that, just as there is sin in the appetite for sin, so there is grace in the desire for grace. There is lowliness in the longing for lowliness; there is meekness in the yearning for meekness; there is purity in the craving for purity. And so a gateway—the largest gateway of all—has been placed in the center of the Western wall for all who, pitifully conscious of their own imperfections, nevertheless covet, and covet passionately, the virtues that they know they lack." (Boreham, *The Heavenly Octave*, 57)

The truth is wonderfully clear. It is not those who are *completely* righteous, not those who are *perfect*, but those who hunger and thirst after righteousness who are blessed.

In the movie *Castaway*, Tom Hanks plays Chuck Noland, a Fed Ex executive stranded on a remote island after a harrowing plane crash. Early in his experience of isolation, Noland begins to feel the effects of lack of food and fresh water. Surrounded by an exquisitely beautiful ocean, he cannot find any drinkable water. He clumsily tries to catch fish, then to spear them, but without much success.

His thirst is so great he licks rainwater off leaves. He becomes so hungry that he eats grubs and insects. As the movie progresses, he realizes that hunger and thirst are his most important concerns—even rescue is secondary to the demands of his body. One of Noland's triumphs is his discovery of inner resources and creativity that enable him to survive. He creates elaborate water-catching devices to assuage his thirst; he masters the skill of spearing fish to alleviate his hunger.

Hunger and thirst are the most basic human yearnings. They can override everything else. Jesus says that God blesses us when we yearn for righteousness with the same kind of intensity that a famished person hunts for something to eat, with the same kind of intensity that motivated Chuck Noland to create water-catching devices to secure drinkable water. The psalmist expressed this yearning: "As a deer longs for flowing streams, so my soul longs for you, O God. My soul thirsts for God, for the living God" (Ps. 42:1-2).

God blesses those who hunger and thirst for righteousness, who yearn to place themselves at the center of God's will, who long for and seek God's righteousness with their whole self—everything within them desires it, everything within them aches for it—not just every now and then but all the time.

Reflecting and Recording

Spend a few minutes reflecting on this word of the keeper of the Martyrs' Gate: "It is one of the fundamental principles of the City of Blessedness that, *just as there is sin in the appetite for sin, so there is grace in the desire for grace*" (emphasis ours).

■ ■ ■

When have you hungered and thirsted for something besides food or water? Briefly describe that experience.

Would you label the just-described experience "religious"? Christian? If not, describe an experience or a season in your life when you specifically hungered and thirsted for God's will and/or a deeper relationship with Christ.

During the Day

Seek awareness of times during the day when your hunger and thirst for righteousness, God's will, and/or God's presence is extraordinary.

DAY 3

Are You Angry Because I Am Kind?

Afascinating story occurs in Matthew's Gospel, chapter 20. A vineyard owner goes out at the beginning of the day and hires workers. He agrees to pay them the normal wage for a day's work. He goes out again about midmorning and hires more workers, agreeing to pay them "whatever is right" (Matt. 20:4). He repeats this process periodically throughout the day until about an hour before the end of the workday, when he goes out one last time and again hires more workers. When it is time to pay his workers, the vineyard owner lines them up, starting with those who began working last, and pays them for a full day's work. When the workers who had worked for an entire day see that those who had come later got paid for a full day, they expect to receive more; after all, they had done the most work. But when their turn comes, they too receive exactly what the vineyard owner promised, a full day's wages. Nor surprisingly, these workers are angry. They should be paid more! They bore the heat of the day, worked the longest; how can it be that those who worked only an hour or so receive the same reward? Here is the vineyard owner's response to these complaints: "Friend, I am doing you no wrong; did you not agree with me for the usual daily wage? Take what belongs to you and go; I choose to give to this last the same as I give to you. Am I not allowed to do what I choose with what belongs to me? Or are you envious because I am generous?" (Matt. 20:13-15).

We hope you can imagine the listeners' astonishment and wonder as Jesus told this story. Our familiarity with this parable shouldn't blind us to its radical nature. The story is radical because it goes against our human tendency to equate justice with merit. It shows the nature of God's grace and righteousness. In contrast to the world, in the kingdom of God everyone will receive the same reward.

One of my favorite movies is *Field of Dreams*. In this film Ray Kinsella (Kevin Costner) feels compelled to create a baseball diamond in the middle of his Iowa cornfield. He doesn't know why he needs to do it, but he keeps hearing a voice saying, "If you build it, they will come"; so he follows his dream. Kinsella tracks down various people who become part of this mystery unfolding in his life: Terence Mann, an author (James Earl Jones), and Dr. "Moonlight" Graham, an elderly doctor who was a former baseball player (Burt Lancaster). Toward the end of the movie, the mysterious players from long ago who have been playing on Ray's field call it a day and head back toward the cornfield, into which they disappear each night. Seemingly on a whim, one of them turns back and asks, "Do you want to come with us?" When Ray realizes that the question is directed at Mann and not at him, he becomes angry. He says, "Why him? I built this field! You wouldn't be here if it weren't for me. . . . I have done everything I've been asked to do. I didn't understand it, but I've done it. And I haven't once asked, 'What's in it for me?'"

As you watch this scene, you empathize with Ray. He *has* hung in there through the long haul, even when he didn't understand what was going on. He *does* deserve to go. We empathize with Ray because we're very much like him, and we're very much like the workers in Jesus' story. We are all alike because we share the same understanding of justice—getting what you deserve. If you work more, you should get more. If you get in line first, you ought to get served first, or get the first choice, or get the best seat. More significantly, this understanding of justice applies not only to our view of the world but to our spiritual lives as well. We believe ourselves to be religious. We believe that we have committed ourselves to the kingdom of God; we are in it for the long haul. But sometimes we can experience an underlying sense of resentment toward God because we feel as though God is being unfair in giving out rewards. We deserve more. We have been working all day.

In this story, Jesus is telling us that we're wrong. God's righteousness is not about getting what we deserve. It is not about working longer or receiving more. Jesus knew that the prevailing hunger and thirst for what the religious people of his day called "righteousness" was really desire for praise. This mock hunger would never be satisfied by their stern, self-deprecating rule keeping and activity designed to impress. The inner craving of the soul can be satisfied only by a joyous righteousness rooted in true love of God and persons, genuinely desiring that God's will be done in the world, and placing ourselves at God's disposal to make it happen.

In God's kingdom we all have the same value and receive the same reward. God does not want to be in relationship with one of us more than another; God wants to be in relationship with all of us. No one is beyond the reach of God's grace. God does not desire to give more of God's kingdom to a few of us; God desires to give all of God's kingdom to all of us; God wants each one of us to share in it. The story of the vineyard owner invites us to *enjoy* God's righteousness rather than compete for it. And the Beatitudes assure us that we will be blessed when we hunger and thirst for righteousness. We'll be blessed when we yearn with our entire being to be in the center of God's will, where all people are valued and lifted up.

Reflecting and Recording

Put yourself in the position of someone in Jesus' story who had worked all day. How would you respond to the vineyard owner's paying all workers the same? Have you ever experienced a similar situation? How might you respond to the owner's question, "Are you envious because I am generous?" Do you tend to equate justice with merit? Spend three or four minutes in reflection. If you want to read the story from scripture, see Matthew 20:1-16.

■ ■ ■

The time line below represents the last ten years of your life. On this time line, plot your hungering and thirsting for God's righteousness. See the line as your "normal" Christian walk. Above the line, mark times when you intensely sought more awareness of God's presence, desired more deeply to do God's will, acted deliberately for peace and justice, or involved yourself intentionally in a program or movement focused on some aspect of God's righteousness in the world.

Below the line, mark those times when you resisted some specific call, became lazy in your quest for righteousness and holiness, or were undisciplined in your devotional life and/or dull in God's presence. Describe two or three experiences you designated above or below the line.

1 ——— 2 ——— 3 ——— 4 ——— 5 ——— 6 ——— 7 ——— 8 ——— 9 ——— 10

During the Day

Observe relationships, actions, and work patterns. Try to discover to what degree merit and reward are connected with people's concept of justice. Seek some examples, however small, of *grace* prevailing over *merit*.

✠

DAY 4

The Law of Gravity

Then Peter said in reply, "Look, we have left everything and followed you. What then will we have?" Jesus said to them, "Truly I tell you, at the renewal of all things, when the Son of Man is seated on the throne of his glory, you who have followed me will also sit on twelve thrones, judging the twelve tribes of Israel. And everyone who has left houses or brothers or sisters or father or mother or children or fields, for my name's sake, will receive a hundredfold, and will inherit eternal life." (Matt. 19:27-30)

If you hold a billiard ball and a marble at the same height and drop them at the same time, which one do you believe will hit the ground first? The billiard ball? It seems logical; after all, it's heavier, so why wouldn't it arrive at the ground faster? Try this experiment. Hold a billiard ball or a bowling ball or whatever heavy object you would like, and a marble or a golf ball or whatever lighter object you would like, at the same height. Now drop them both at the same time. What did you discover? You discovered the law of gravity. Regardless of their weight or size, objects fall to the ground at the same speed. For some of us, this truth causes quite a bit of wonder!

We often respond to the story of the vineyard owner (discussed yesterday) with the same wonder. Sometimes we find it surprising that God's grace and righteousness do not relate to what people deserve or how much work they've done. God's grace and righteousness are more like the law of gravity—they treat everyone equally. No matter how heavy we are, no matter how much weight we believe we carry, we all still arrive at the same time.

This is a crucial truth as we seek to claim Jesus' promise of blessing. It is the crucial truth that motivated Jesus to eat with sinners and tax collectors. It is why he invited them to enter the kingdom just like the Pharisees. God's "law of gravity" is what Jesus hinted at when he said that the last will be first and the first will be last (Matt. 20:16)—not ranking but the first and the last getting the same thing. God desires the same for all of us because in God's eyes we are all valuable.

Recently an art exhibit in Lafayette took place in the local theater, which had been empty and in disrepair for many years. Fifteen artists installed pieces that fit in to the context of the theater. In other words, each artist created a work of art in response to an idea received from the theater itself. These installations were displayed throughout the building. A friend of mine created a powerful piece in the theater balcony.

Like many theaters across the United States, at one time this theater in Indiana was segregated—whites sat on the main floor, while people of color were relegated to the balcony. When I arrived in the balcony to view my friend's artwork, the first thing I noticed was images of people projected on the backs of various seats, as though they were sitting enjoying a theater production. As I stood and watched, the images changed so that many different kinds of people were shown sitting in the balcony. After a while I realized that none of the changing images were people of color; in fact there were three images that never changed—all of them people of color. These three people remained in their seats, never changing, while all kinds of change was going on around them.

This artistic creation affected me significantly. I thought about how time has passed—our theaters aren't segregated anymore—but people are still locked in the cycle of injustice. My mind kept returning to the images of all those people coming and going, and then to those three static images, forever constrained to their place in the balcony.

If God's righteousness resembles the law of gravity, it doesn't matter how much weight you pull in the world, you will still arrive at the same time as everyone else. That means that what God wants for us, God also wants for others—all others—even those we don't care for or understand, even those we smugly think aren't pulling as much weight. The reverse is also true. If God's righteousness resembles the law of gravity, then the words of an old blues tune ring true: "None of us is free if one of us is chained." If even one person remains relegated to the balcony, then we all are relegated there. If we do not hunger and thirst for the day when no one has to sit in the balcony, then we will surely miss out on God's blessing.

For God's kingdom to be fully realized, we must live God's law of gravity—live out the reality that we all are of great value. God desires that we all share in God's kingdom. If we want to claim God's blessing, if we truly want to be satisfied as Jesus promises, we must hunger and thirst for righteousness. We must be consumed with the mission of doing right and seeing God's rightness become a living reality. We have to struggle for that as vigorously as we struggle for air when we get the wind knocked out of us.

Reflecting and Recording

Recall a cultural practice or a personal experience where persons were relegated to lesser places or denied benefits. What were the reasons? Make some notes here.

Spend a few minutes reflecting on this statement: None of us is free if one of us is chained.

■ ■ ■

During Week Eight we will deal with the issue of persecution. Are persons in your state, city, or community persecuted because of ethnic or sexual identity, age, education, economic, or cultural circumstances? Who are they? What does it mean to hunger and thirst for righteousness in these circumstances? Spend a few minutes reflecting on these issues.

■ ■ ■

Close your time of reflection by praying these words from Psalm 63:

> O God, you are my God, I seek you.
>   my soul thirsts for you;
> my flesh faints for you,
>   as in a dry and weary land where there is no water.
> So I have looked upon you in the sanctuary,
>   beholding your power and glory.
> Because your steadfast love is better than life,
>   my lips will praise you.
> So I will bless you as long as I live;
>   I will lift up my hands and call on your name.
>
> My soul is satisfied as with a rich feast,
>   and my mouth praises you with joyful lips
> when I think of you on my bed, and meditate on you
>   in the watches of the night:
> for you have been my help
>   and in the shadow of your wings I sing for joy.
> My soul clings to you;
>   your right hand upholds me.

During the Day

The above prayer is printed on page 211. Cut it out and use it as a mealtime prayer, alone, with family, or with friends.

DAY 5

More Than Pity

Blessed are the merciful, for they will receive mercy. (Matt. 5:7)

All the Beatitudes are connected. The fullness of their claim is cumulative. Clarence Jordan calls them "steps into the kingdom," with each growing out of the other. In the same sense, F. W. Boreham said:

> The only mercifulness that is strong and steadfast and reliable is that which has come along the lines indicated in the Beatitudes. The heart that has been reduced to a beautiful poverty of spirit; the heart that has mourned in lowliest contrition; the heart that has learned the subtle secret of meekness; the heart that has hungered and thirsted after righteousness—such a heart is alone qualified to exhibit mercy in its tenderest and most effective forms. (Boreham, *The Heavenly Octave*, 68)

Today we move to Jesus' fifth promise of blessing, to those who are merciful. What a powerful and much needed word for our world today. Notice that Jesus makes this promise directly on the heels of his promise to the righteous. Those who hunger and thirst for righteousness will be filled, and those who are merciful will receive mercy.

As we reflect on this Beatitude, we assert that mercifulness is essentially a Christian grace. A casual comparison between countries that have been significantly shaped by Christianity and those that have not reveals a wide gulf in the value placed upon persons: how they are treated and protected. The world would have been a pitiless place had Jesus not come. Neglect, exposure, and even murder of newborn babies were common practices in the world to which Jesus came—even amid the philosophy of Rome and the culture of Greece. The chief amusement of Roman society, even in all its pomp and glory, was the fighting of men, and of men with wild beasts. The obligation to show consideration and pity to strangers and even enemies became a primary plank in the platform of Christian understanding of relationships. Hospitals, schools, orphanages, homes for the poor, and similar institutions are monuments marking the presence of Christian mercy in every culture. Indeed, mercy is essentially a Christian grace.

While millions of persons who make no Christian profession perform deeds of mercy every day, and revolting cruelty toward humankind may take place in the misunderstood name of Christ, to be merciful is an explicitly Christian call, and the quality of mercy that seems dominant in Christian culture is a result of the spirit of Jesus working in generations of his followers.

This Beatitude is integral to a Christian understanding of human value and relationships. Dr. Boone Bowen, one of my favorite seminary teachers, made this memorably clear to me in his lectures on central words in the Old Testament message. One of those words was *chesedh*. I can still hear his deep voice and the way he spoke this word in the language he loved. Though he said *chesedh* is untranslatable, it is the Hebrew word for *mercy*. The Greek word for *mercy* is *eleos*, and as we have it in the New Testament, it is traced back to *chesedh*. It does not mean only "to sympathize," in the common sense of the word; it is not simply to feel sorry for someone in trouble. The meaning of the Hebrew word is much deeper; according to William Barclay, *chesedh* implies "the ability to get right inside the other person's skin," or as the Native Americans would say, "to walk in another [person's] moccasins." Barclay notes that this means we identify so closely with another that we see with her eyes, think thoughts with his mind, and feel emotions with her feelings."

Mercy demands intention, deliberate effort—an act of the will. Perhaps the most dramatic act of mercy in the New Testament is Jesus' response to the leper who came asking for healing. (See Matthew 8:1-4.) Leprosy was a physically devastating disease, reducing a human being to a hideous wreck. It was a horrific experience in which a person died by inches. The mental anguish and social banishment were as bad or worse than the physical suffering. Josephus mentioned that lepers were treated "as if in effect they were dead men." (Barclay, *The Gospel of Matthew*, rev. ed., 1:295) When persons were diagnosed with leprosy, they were immediately banished from human society. Religiously they were considered unclean. "As long as the disease lasts, they will be ceremonially unclean and must live in isolation outside the camp" (Lev. 13:46, NLT).

To the Jews, the defilement associated with coming into contact with a leper was second only to that of touching a dead body. Even the air around a leper was considered unclean. In the time of Jesus, lepers were barred from Jerusalem or any town with a wall; they were to shout loudly, "Unclean, unclean" wherever they went so as to give others time to avoid them.

In light of these facts, the story in Matthew 8 is intriguing. A leper came to Jesus, knelt before him, and spoke: "Lord, if you choose, you can make me clean" (Matt. 8:2). Don't you wonder about this radical violation of custom and religious law—a leper coming into the presence of another person? What courage and confidence on the part of the leper! What emboldened his radical action? Undoubtedly he had heard enough about Jesus to believe that Jesus would welcome one whom everyone else would drive away. Even in his bold confidence and courage, the leper demonstrated reverence and humility. He knelt before Jesus, but he did not demand healing. He expressed bold faith, but humility obviously inspired Jesus' response. "Lord," the leper said, "if you want to, you can make me well again."

I like Jesus' response as rendered in the New Living Translation: "Jesus touched him. 'I want to,' he said. 'Be healed!'" (Matt. 8:3). There was no hesitation. Jesus touched him, and the leper was healed.

Responding to the leper was an act of the will on Jesus' part, an act of compassionate mercy. He did what others dared not do. He looked at the man, *saw him*, acknowledged him as a living human being, and responded to him as a person, not as a maimed, disfigured piece of flesh. He *listened* to him, *touched* him, and *spoke* to him, three action responses that no one else dared make.

In this story and throughout his life, Jesus rescued the word *mercy* from mere acts of pity such as proudly putting a coin into a beggar's cup or serving a meal to the homeless on Thanksgiving Day. The kind of mercy Jesus says is blessed is an attitude of compassion toward all persons that causes us to desire to share gladly what we have. We want to do whatever we can to make their lives, if not rich and meaningful, at least bearable, with enough hope to keep them going.

Reflecting and Recording

Recall and briefly describe here the last genuine act of mercy you saw someone perform. When did it occur? Who was merciful to whom? What does this incident say about the pervasiveness and quality of mercy in our day?

Reread the last paragraph in today's text. What would it mean for you to be merciful according to this understanding?

During the Day

Look for persons who show mercy today—and for opportunities to show mercy. Continue praying the prayer from Psalm 63.

✠

DAY 6

As Far as the East Is from the West

Mercy is an attribute of God. The psalmist makes that very clear:

Bless the LORD, O my soul,
and all that is within me, bless his holy name.
Bless the LORD, O my soul, and do not forget all his benefits—
who forgives all your iniquity,
who heals all your diseases,
who redeems your life from the Pit,
who crowns you with steadfast love and mercy,
who satisfies you with good as long as you live
so that your youth is renewed like the eagle's.

. . . .

For as the heavens are high above the earth,
so great is his steadfast love toward those who fear him;
as far as the east is from the west,
so far he removes our transgressions from us. (Ps. 103:1-5, 11-12)

Likewise, mercy is something God requires of us. "He has told you, O mortal, what is good; and what does the LORD require of you but to do justice, and to love kindness, and to walk humbly with your God?" (Mic. 6:8).

Mercy (*chesedh*) is one of the great words of the old covenant; Christ uses this word to declare boldly an aspect of the new covenant: "Be merciful, just as your Father is merciful" (Luke 6:36). Mercy is the attribute that Jesus commended in the story of the good Samaritan (Luke 10:37). The Samaritan had mercy on the man who had been beaten and robbed. Jesus designates mercy as one of the "weightier matters of the law." "Woe to you, scribes and Pharisees, hypocrites! For you tithe mint, dill, and cummin, and have neglected the weightier matters of the law: justice and mercy and faith. It is these you ought to have practiced without neglecting the others" (Matt. 23:23). He identifies mercy with forgiveness (in the parable of the unforgiving servant, Matt. 18:23-35) and says that if we lack forgiveness, we will not receive mercy.

The mercy Jesus speaks of is always active; it is sympathy in action—pity and compassion expressed in gracious deeds. In his most descriptive word about judgment, Jesus said that our level of mercy is what will determine our place within or outside of the kingdom. (See Matthew 25:31-46.)

Mercy is the active expression of our seeing others not as beggars to whom we might give but as brothers and sisters with whom we share. Again, it is a condition of heart required of those who love God: "How does God's love abide in anyone who has the world's goods and sees a brother or sister in need and yet refuses help?" (1 John 3:17).

Return to our beginning claim: Mercy is an attribute of God. We must first understand what it means for God to be merciful before we can understand how to be merciful toward others. Most dictionaries define *mercy* as kind and compassionate treatment. But as we have seen in scripture, the second part of that definition remains key to our understanding of mercy, because mercy does not involve just kindness. In the Bible, mercy is always associated with forgiveness. God's mercy, then, does not involve just kindness but also forgiveness. God's mercy is God's act of wiping the slate clean, separating us from our sin and wrongdoing *as far as the east is from the west.*

God's mercy acts as a powerful force in our lives. It transforms and re-creates us, saying that yesterday does not eternally haunt us; we become new people today. God's mercy forever alters our destiny, transforming Mary Magdalene from a woman of questionable reputation into an example of precious, holy love, destined to be the first witness to our Lord's resurrection; moving Simon Peter from cowardice to legendary leader; and transforming Paul from persecuting skeptic to powerful messenger of the gospel.

The discovery of God's mercy is a transforming experience. When we hear of God's power to separate us from our wrongdoing as far as the east is from the west, we receive good news. But discovering God's mercy can also be painful, because experiencing that power involves honesty with God. We must admit our wrongdoing before God can separate us from it.

In Acts 2, Peter preaches to a crowd, laying before them the gospel of Jesus and confronting them with the fact that they were the ones who crucified him. Peter's words deeply convict the crowd, and they respond with the earnest question, "What should we do?" That question is key to experiencing God's mercy—when we are honest with God about who we are and what we've done, we then need to ask God, "What do I do now?" Peter answers the question: We must turn from our sins, turn to God, and be baptized in the name of Jesus Christ so that our sins can be forgiven (Acts 2:38). Eugene Peterson has paraphrased Peter's call to repentance like this: "Now it's time to change your ways! Turn to face God so he can wipe away your sins, pour out showers of blessing to refresh you" (Acts 3:19-20, *The Message*).

God's mercy is a shower of blessing that cleanses, transforms, and refreshes us, and we experience it by turning to God. As we turn to God, we begin to grow as "imitators" of God, and the Beatitude comes alive in us: as we are merciful, we receive mercy. As already indicated, when Jesus talked about judgment and the life beyond, he singled out mercy—or the lack of it—as the determining factor of our ultimate destiny (Matt. 25:31-46; Luke 16:19-31). Please notice that this is not "merit" theology—making a claim on God's mercy because of our deeds. We simply must practice mercy as we seek to be like God.

> And if on Judgment Day the merciful man hears the verdict, "Come, ye blessed of my Father," it will not be because he has "made out, and reckoned on his ways, and bargained for his love," but because, all unconsciously, he has acted like him of whom it is written, "as is his majesty, so also is his mercy." (Hunter, *A Pattern for Life*, 39)

Reflecting and Recording

Name three persons you know who most faithfully practice mercy.

List words or phrases describing these persons.

What characteristics of these persons are most absent from your life? Make some notes.

Spend a few minutes reflecting on this claim: Since mercy is identified with forgiveness, *if we lack mercy, we will not receive mercy and forgiveness.*

■ ■ ■

Spend the rest of your time in prayer, confessing and repenting if need be, claiming this promise: God's mercy is God's act of wiping the slate clean, separating us from our sin and wrongdoing *as far as the east is from the west.*

During the Day

Call or write the persons you named as merciful. Thank them and tell them what a blessing their witness is.

Deliberately seek to live today by Jesus' admonition "Be merciful, just as your Father is merciful" (Luke 6:36).

Continue to use the prayer from Psalm 63.

DAY 7

The Mercy of the King

Let no evil talk come out of your mouths, but only what is useful for building up, as there is need, so that your words may give grace to those who hear. And do not grieve the Holy Spirit of God, with which you were marked with a seal for the day of redemption. Put away from you all bitterness and wrath and anger and wrangling and slander, together with all malice, and be kind to one another, tenderhearted, forgiving one another, as God in Christ has forgiven you. (Eph. 4:29-32)

If Jesus calls us to a life marked by mercy and forgiveness, if Jesus promises that we will be blessed when we practice that kind of living, it behooves us to understand what forgiveness actually is. Forgiveness is neither bitterness nor denial. It is an unflinching acknowledgment that a wrong has been committed. It is an honest, direct recognition of the suffering that has been experienced. And then it involves letting go and starting fresh—sometimes again and again. We can understand that concept with our minds, but it is never as easy to practice forgiveness. That is why in Matthew 18 Jesus told the story of a king who decided to get his financial affairs in order; he wanted to give us an illustration of true forgiveness.

Jesus said that the king, in getting his affairs in order, discovered that a servant owed him ten thousand talents. That was a lot of money! It could be compared to owing the IRS millions of dollars—an amount we could never dream of being able to repay. When the king discovers this great debt, he has the servant hauled into his court and tells him to pay up or he and his entire family and all their possessions will be sold. Obviously the man can't pay, so he throws himself at the king's feet and begs for mercy. "Please be patient! I'll do everything I can! I'm begging you, please!" The king is touched. He truly feels empathy for the servant, so he releases him and forgives his debt.

For those of you who are familiar with this story, the amount this man owed may seem unimportant; we usually view the rest of the story as holding the significant meaning. But the truth is, the immensity of this man's debt actually has great consequence when we're talking about mercy. As we hear Jesus' words, we might want to put ourselves in this man's place and ask if there is any debt in our lives we could never dream of repaying.

The story continues as Jesus says that the man leaves the king's court, jubilant with the experience of mercy he has just received. On his way out, he happens to run into another man who owes him money—one hundred denarii. This too is a significant amount of money; yet the ability to repay this debt is not unfathomable. One denarius per day was a normal wage in that time, so the second man owed about sixteen weeks' worth of pay. Certainly that is a substantial amount to owe, but it was nothing compared with the first man's debt. Unfortunately, the first man, who has just experienced remarkable mercy, demands immediate payment. The second man knows he cannot repay, so he falls at the first man's feet, pleading for patience. "I will repay you! I will work off the entire debt! Please have mercy!" But the first man refuses to listen and has him thrown in jail.

As in much of life, this incident does not go unnoticed. The other servants witness the first man's lack of understanding. They know how merciful the king was to forgive his debt and are offended by the man's lack of compassion, so they inform the king of what happened. The king, outraged, brings the first man before him and rages at his lack of gratitude and compassion, asking him, "Should you not have had mercy on your fellow slave, as I had mercy on you?" (Matt. 18:33). The king is so angry that he withdraws his offer of mercy and hands over the servant to the jailers to be tortured until he can repay every penny of his debt, which we can assume resulted in a life sentence, considering how much the man owed.

You can probably surmise the point Jesus made in this story. Forgiveness is unlimited. God willingly extends mercy even in cases where the debt cannot possibly be repaid. Forgiveness is unlimited, and the experience of giving and receiving cannot be separated. It is spiritually dangerous to accept forgiveness for ourselves and not extend it to others. Even more significant is the truth that we risk not receiving forgiveness if we do not give it to others. The spiritual danger of separating the giving and receiving of forgiveness is emphasized not only by Jesus' promise in the Beatitudes, but also by the way Jesus taught us to pray. When we pray the Lord's Prayer, we say, "Forgive us our trespasses (debts), as we forgive those who trespass against us (our debtors)." The truth is clear and unavoidable: The blessing of this Beatitude does not come to those who are quick to suspect, swift to condemn, and slow to forgive. If we are to experience Jesus' promise of blessing and mercy, we must dedicate ourselves to living a life of forgiveness.

Reflecting and Recording

Charles Haddon Spurgeon offered this cryptic summary of our life with God and others: "What we are to others, God will be to us." (Connell, comp., *The Secret of Happiness*, 26) Spend a few minutes reflecting on this claim. Is it a new idea? Do you believe it to be true? Do you live as though you believe it is true?

■ ■ ■

Read Jesus' word from Matthew 25:31-46. Spend three or four minutes now reflecting on the connection between Jesus' word, "As you did it to one of the least of these . . . , you did it to me," and Spurgeon's claim, "What we are to others, God will be to us."

■ ■ ■

During the Day

Engage someone in a discussion of Spurgeon's word, "What we are to others, God will be to us." Tell where these words came from, in other words, your involvement with the Beatitudes of Jesus, how the word challenges you, and ask how this person responds to the word.

✠

Group Meeting
for Week Five

Introduction

The disciplines needed for prayerful living—praying without ceasing, or living in a continual state of prayer—are *intention* and *attention*. These disciplines are also necessary for meaningful group sharing. We must pay attention to what is going on around us.

In group settings the easy route is laziness. Individual group members may be tempted to "play it safe" and not risk honesty and vulnerability.

Energy is another issue. Listening and speaking demand physical and emotional energy. So the temptation is to hold back, to be only half present, and to fail to invest the attention and focus essential for full participation.

We urge you to withstand these temptations. These sharing sessions are important. Don't underestimate the value of each person's contribution.

Sharing Together

1.   Begin your time together with prayer by the group leader or someone else (consulted ahead of time). Then sing a chorus or a couple of verses of a familiar hymn.

2.   Ask each person to share the most challenging and meaningful insight or experience during this week.

3.   Invite two or three people to name and describe the most righteous person they know.

4.   Spend eight to ten minutes discussing righteousness as "desiring God's will to be done in the world, and . . . placing ourselves at God's disposal in order to make that happen." Refer to the persons described as righteous—do they fit the description? Call to mind other people who do.

5.   Invite as many as will to share their rendition of the sentence "Just as there is sin in the appetite for sin, so there is grace in the desire for grace" as they recorded in Reflecting and Recording on Day 2. Then spend a few minutes discussing the implications of this claim.

6.   Invite one or two persons to share one of their most intense experiences of hungering and thirsting for God's will and/or a deeper relationship with Christ.

7.   On Day 4 participants were asked to observe whether any people remain locked in the cycle of injustice. Spend a few minutes with individuals sharing their response.

8.   Invite two or three people to describe the last genuine act of mercy they saw someone perform.

9.   Spend eight to ten minutes discussing the claim that "mercifulness is essentially a Christian grace," thinking about how different cultures value persons and about the difference Christ has made in culture.

10.   Jesus' threefold response to the leper (discussed in Day 5) was that he saw him, touched him, and spoke to him. Consider your community. What persons or groups need this kind of attention? What ministries of your congregation express genuine mercy? Spend eight to ten minutes in this discussion.

11.   Spend eight to ten minutes discussing the claim that mercy is an attribute of God and expresses itself in forgiveness. If forgiveness is how God expresses mercy, what does this require of us? How do you think and feel about the statement that "if we lack mercy we will not receive mercy and forgiveness"?

12.   Spend the balance of your time discussing ways we most often fail to be merciful.

Praying Together

Sharing the prayers of our hearts with others not only confirms our prayerful desires and claims but also inspires the prayers of others and adds the "two-or-three-agreeing" condition for answered prayer (Matt. 18:19-20). Spend your prayer time by allowing those who are willing to offer brief prayers growing out of your sharing. As you begin, ask if anyone has specific prayer requests. When as many as wish have prayed, close by inviting all to pray together the Lord's Prayer.

Week Six

Pure in Heart

DAY 1

Clean Hands and Pure Hearts

Blessed are the pure in heart, for they will see God. (Matt. 5:8)

Our mother and grandmother, Cora Dunnam, was ready to "cross over to Jordan" long before God chose to take her. In the latter part of her life, Grandma Corie, or Co-bell, as so many called her, often talked about being ready to die and finally seeing God face-to-face. One of her favorite psalms was Psalm 24, especially verses 3-4:

Who shall ascend the hill of the LORD?
    And who shall stand in his holy place?
Those who have clean hands and pure hearts,
    who do not lift up their souls to what is false,
    and do not swear deceitfully.

When she recited this psalm and arrived at those verses, she would stop, lift her hands, and say with a broad smile of assurance, "I've got clean hands." She was ready to see God.

Who is worthy to stand in God's presence? In the sixth Beatitude, Jesus said the pure in heart "will see God." Centuries before, the psalmist had answered this question with, "Those who have clean hands and pure hearts."

Jesus accused the Pharisees of his day of cleaning "the outside of the cup and of the dish, but inside you are full of greed and wickedness" (Luke 11:39). He was making the point that a harmony must exist between the condition of our heart and our outward actions.

My friend Jim Harnish puts it this way: "The heart of the matter is always a matter of the heart."

The word "heart" appears 592 times in scripture. You could say that the Bible is one long, divinely inspired electrocardiogram. In scripture, the heart represents the life-giving core of human life. It's like the "mission control center" in Houston that guides the space shuttle in its orbit. The heart is the motivating, controlling center of our human personality, the deep inner source of passion, energy, and direction for our lives. The writer of the Old Testament book of Proverbs captures the overall importance of this theme when he challenges us to "keep your heart with all vigilance, for from it flow the springs of life" (Proverbs 4:23). With unwavering clarity, the scriptures take us to the deepest places of the heart, convinced that the heart of the matter is always a matter of the heart. (Harnish, *You Only Have to Die*, 13–14)

Life on earth is a progression, a process of soul and character development from birth to death, a long journey that begins with our entrance into the world and ends when we leave it to stand before God. Because life is a process of soul and character development, "the heart of the matter is always a matter of the heart." Our heart is of the utmost importance because from it flows our character. We may have a brave heart, a faint heart, a gentle heart, a cheating heart, a tender heart, a cheerful heart, a deceitful heart, a generous heart, or a hard heart. The heart is the *center of our emotions*—we may be cold-hearted or warm, passionate or indifferent. Our heart influences our will as we steel our heart for a particular decision, and it's the *seat of our moral integrity*. Jesus used the tree and its fruit as a metaphor for our lives:

> No good tree bears bad fruit, nor again does a bad tree bear good fruit; for each tree is known by its own fruit. Figs are not gathered from thorns, nor are grapes picked from a bramble bush. The good person out of the good treasure of the heart produces good, and the evil person out of evil treasure produces evil; for it is out of the abundance of the heart that the mouth speaks. (Luke 6:43-45)

Notice that he connected action flowing from the condition of our heart with the tree bearing fruit. On the journey of life everything is a matter of the heart, for from it issues the good, the bad, and everything in between. That truth alone is enough to make our heart extremely important, but there is more. Our heart is the dwelling place of Christ through the power of the Holy Spirit. So, the condition of our heart is extremely significant. Who will ascend the hill of the Lord and stand in his holy place? Those who have clean hands and pure hearts. God blesses the pure in heart; they are the ones who will see God.

Reflecting and Recording

Reflect on the condition of your heart. Put a check (✓) by any of the following words that might currently describe your heart.

_____ brave	_____ faint	_____ gentle
_____ deceitful	_____ generous	_____ cheating
_____ tender	_____ hard	_____ cheerful

Select two characteristics you checked—one positive, one negative—and make some notes on how the condition of your heart affects your actions.

During the Day

Psalm 24:3-4 is printed on page 209. Cut out and display these verses where you will see them often during the day. Read and reread them until you have memorized them. Pay close attention to how the characteristics of your heart that you checked above, positive and negative, determine your actions today.

DAY 2

An Undivided Nature

In the beginning was the Word, and the Word was with God, and the Word was God. He was in the beginning with God. All things came into being through him, and without him not one thing came into being. What has come into being in him was life, and the life was the light of all people. The light shines in the darkness, and the darkness did not overcome it. (John 1:1-5)

Light and dark cannot coexist. If light is present, then darkness can't be; if we are surrounded by darkness, then there is no light. The Gospel of John tells us that Jesus Christ is the means through which God gave light to the world. Therefore, wherever the light of Christ shines, there can be no darkness. Yesterday we mentioned that our heart is the dwelling place of Christ through the power of the Holy Spirit, which makes its condition of utmost importance. If we are to welcome Christ into our heart, we can have no darkness there. We must choose the light or the dark, for they cannot exist together.

Who will ascend to the hill of the Lord and stand in his holy place? Those with clean hands and pure hearts. The condition of our heart determines whether we will see God. "Blessed are the pure in heart, for they will see God." The Greek word for *pure, katharos,* is used in many different ways. Originally, it simply meant clean, and was used, for instance, to describe once-dirty clothes that had been washed clean. Years ago there was a laundry soap named Pure, and often advertisements for laundry and dish detergents will use the word *pure*. Until it merged with another company, there was once a huge company called Pure Oil. The company was sending the message that its products had been refined until no foreign elements were present.

Other meanings of the Greek word for *pure* included the winnowing or sifting of grain to clean off the chaff. Barclay reminds us that the Greek word *katharos* appeared often with another adjective, *akeratos*, used to describe milk or wine that is "unadulterated with water, or of metal which has in it no tinge of alloy." (Barclay, *The Gospel of Matthew*, rev. ed., 1:106)

No wonder then that Webster's dictionary says something is pure if it has a "homogeneous or uniform composition, not mixed." (*Webster's II: New College Dictionary*, s.v. "pure") Purity involves having a singleness of nature. It is about being undiluted or full-strength. Time and again Jesus rebuked the Pharisees for their hypocrisy, their pretense. This Beatitude suggests that God blesses us when our hearts are undivided.

Unfortunately, we all know how difficult it is to achieve such a state; our hearts are anything but undivided. This truth is demonstrated for most of us every time we come to our prayer and devotional time. We seek to stay centered, but we find our minds running off in myriad directions. We read scripture but discover that what we have read hasn't registered. We attempt to pray for particular persons and needs but find ourselves thinking of what we must do during the day. More often than not, our minds are full of things other than what we intend to be mindful of.

Perhaps at a more debilitating or even destructive level, our hearts are divided in our commitments and loyalties. Few of us move through many days without moral compromise. Reflecting on our life struggle, we confess with Paul, "I do not do the good I want, but the evil I do not want is what I do" (Rom. 7:19). The painful honesty of such confession was expressed by Alexander Whyte, one of the great Scottish preachers of another generation:

> A traveling evangelist came to Edinburgh and set up his tent. One of the ways he attracted attention and caused enough stir for the curious was by criticizing other preachers. He made a harsh attack upon a Dr. Wilson who was an outstanding Edinburgh minister and a friend of Alexander Whyte. A parishioner reported to Dr. Whyte:
>
> "Pastor, I went to hear the evangelist last night. He said your friend, Dr. Wilson, is not a truly converted man."
>
> Whyte leaped from his chair, eyes blazing. "That rascal!" he shouted. "How dare he. Wilson is a converted man or no one is!"
>
> The parishioner was shocked; he had never seen his pastor angry. "But, Dr. Whyte, that isn't all. The evangelist said you are not a converted man."
>
> This took the fire out of Dr. Whyte. He wilted back into his chair, slowly put his face into his hands. For a while there was silence. Then with an awful earnestness he said, "Leave me, my friend. I must examine my heart." (Dunnam, *Be Your Whole Self*, 46–47)

Dr. Whyte knew, as we must learn, that we cannot remain inattentive to our hearts—to what stirs and grows there in the depths.

Reflecting and Recording

Under each of the psalmist's characteristics of those who "ascend the hill of the LORD," write words or phrases that concretely express or describe those characteristics:

Clean Hands   **Pure Heart**

Put a check (✓) by those expressions or descriptions that are missing from your life. Put an X by those that have some reality in your life.

Pray that God will empower you in your commitment to have clean hands and a pure heart.

During the Day

Continue memorizing Psalm 24:3-4. Read or speak these verses aloud as often as possible today.

Pay attention to your actions and attitudes today: do they reflect clean hands and a pure heart?

DAY 3

Inside Truth

Have mercy on me, O God,
    according to your steadfast love;
    according to your abundant mercy blot out my transgressions.
Wash me thoroughly from my iniquity, and cleanse me from my sin.

For I know my transgressions, and my sin is ever before me.
Against you, you alone, have I sinned,
    and done what is evil in your sight,

> so that you are justified in your sentence
>   and blameless when you pass judgment.
> Indeed, I was born guilty,
>   a sinner when my mother conceived me.
>
> You desire truth in the inward being;
>   therefore teach me wisdom in my secret heart.
> Purge me with hyssop, and I shall be clean;
>   wash me, and I shall be whiter than snow.
> Let me hear joy and gladness;
>   let the bones that you have crushed rejoice.
> Hide your face from my sins, and blot out all my iniquities.
>
> Create in me a clean heart, O God,
>   and put a new and right spirit within me.
> Do not cast me away from your presence,
>   and do not take your holy spirit from me.
> Restore to me the joy of your salvation,
>   and sustain in me a willing spirit. (Ps. 51:1-12)

Ancient editors say that Psalm 51 is King David's anguished cry for forgiveness and cleansing after he faced up to his blatant sin with Bathsheba. The prophet Nathan had confronted David with his lust, adultery, intrigue, pretense, and sham. He reminded David of how he had schemed to have his trusted servant Uriah murdered. The king of Israel had deliberately broken five of the Ten Commandments.

David had no escape; the secret was out. Yet as we read the psalm, we feel some relief. The hidden deed had surfaced. The cancer that had eaten away at David's soul was now exposed and labeled for what it was. His need for subterfuge and deception was over.

David knew the ramifications of a divided heart. He was full of contradiction: loving God, yet committing adultery and murder. Nevertheless, he knew he had to be honest with God in order for God to heal, forgive, and transform him. And so he owned up to all he had done. The truth of this statement penetrated his soul: "You desire truth in the inward being." *Truth inside* is essential, so David cried, "Create in me a clean heart, O God, and put a new and right spirit within me" (v. 10).

Peeling back the layers of our heart is not easy. Uncovering the hidden parts can be painful. No easy, quick fixes exist for a divided heart. Changing the heart requires hard work and openness to the transforming work of God.

This passage is not a deliberate reflection on the nature of sin and moral responsibility. It is the tortured cry of a sensitive spirit, an outburst of emotion expressing the deepest yearnings of the soul. We may think David tries to rationalize his own actions or seeks to evade responsibility when he says, "I was born guilty, a sinner when my mother conceived me" (v. 5). But if he thinks for a moment that he has an excuse, that thought soon leaves him as he faces the spectacle he has made of himself. Standing before the mirror of his soul, he sees himself in every repugnant detail.

"Purge me with hyssop." Hyssop was an aromatic oil sprinkled on lepers and the loathsome sick.

"Wash me, and I shall be whiter than snow." David speaks as if his garments are filthy; thus he shares the sharpness of his self-rebuke and the degradation he feels.

"Let the bones that you have crushed rejoice." His bones were not literally broken; yet he was spiritually broken, and someone with a broken spirit cannot stand upright.

"Hide your face from my sins." David sees himself as so repulsive that he is afraid God will completely recoil from him if God looks upon him before the process of cleansing makes him presentable again.

Don't let these images throw you. David, looking at himself, described what he saw. All of us do not see the same way, for we are not the same people. Yet each of us has a soul-reflection. Some of us never look at it, but we need to.

In the mirror of your soul, what do you see? Pride, deception, lust, self-righteousness, wasted talent, callousness toward the needs of others, idolatry (for example, making a god out of your money, security, or self-image), cheating, lying, complacency in light of human suffering and moral decay, neurotic fear, failure to develop gifts God has given you, an exaggerated ego that puts down others and puffs up self? What do you see?

"Blessed are the pure in heart." Blessed are those who open themselves to the pain of honesty and invite God to have mercy, to create a new heart within them.

Reflecting and Recording

Spend some time reflecting upon and making the following petitions of David your prayer:

"Against you, you alone, have I sinned."

■ ■ ■

"Wash me thoroughly from my iniquity, and cleanse me from my sin."

■ ■ ■

"I know my transgressions, and my sin is ever before me." I name them now (note your transgressions in this space).

"Create in me a clean heart, O God, and put a new and right spirit within me."

"Do not cast me away from your presence, and do not take your holy spirit from me."

"Restore to me the joy of your salvation."

During the Day

These petitions are printed on page 209. Cut out the affirmation card, carry it with you, and pray David's petitions three or four times today.

DAY 4

A Forgiving Heart

Pray then in this way:
    Our Father in heaven,
    hallowed be your name.
    Your kingdom come.
    Your will be done,
        on earth as it is in heaven.
    Give us this day our daily bread.
    And forgive us our debts,
        as we also have forgiven our debtors.
    And do not bring us to the time of trial,
        but rescue us from the evil one.
For if you forgive others their trespasses, your heavenly Father will also forgive you; but if you do not forgive others, neither will your Father forgive your trespasses. (Matt. 6:9-15)

On Day 1 we talked about our mother and grandmother raising her hands in response to Psalm 24. She could raise her hands and proclaim, "I've got clean hands" not because she thought she was perfect, sinless, or pure but because she knew she was forgiven. Scripture doesn't stop with the assertion that all humans are sinful. It continues with the good news that our sinful nature has been redeemed. God is faithful. If we are honest with God, confess our sins, and repent, God offers forgiveness and cleansing. Confession, repentance, and forgiveness, then, are part of an integral process of our journey toward God. This process is how we move ever closer to a pure heart.

It seems natural that we would embrace this process, willingly and gladly coming before God with our struggles, failings, and faults; but that doesn't seem to be the case. Instead we bury those things, hiding them so that no one, especially God, can see them.

A television commercial airing frequently these days shows a young man watching TV in his apartment. The apartment is an absolute mess. Dirty clothes and dishes are everywhere; sports equipment, soda pop cans, candy wrappers, and empty potato chip bags are piled on top of everything else. A young woman knocks on his door, and we see him frantically looking around, clearly wanting to invite her in but distressed about the state of his apartment. As we watch the young woman standing at the door, we hear the young man say, "Just a minute!" and a few loud bangs and crunches later, he opens the door and leads her into his spotless apartment. She's impressed with his apartment, and as he goes to the kitchen she takes off her coat and opens the closet door, only to be creamed by all the junk that comes flying out.

My house is cleaned weekly, but no matter how hard I try, there's always a closet or drawer or corner somewhere that ends up piled with junk. The junk consists of everything I don't have time to deal with in the process of cleaning. We all have places like that. We procrastinate in deciding what to keep and what to throw away because it's easier to just throw stuff into a junk drawer or closet. But that approach only lasts so long; eventually we can't open the drawer or closet without getting creamed by all the stuff inside.

Our hearts are the same way. We keep cramming things inside that we don't want anyone else to see—attitudes, passions, desires, behaviors. Eventually something happens and all that junk we've tried to stuff inside us comes flying out, often wounding us and those around us.

God desires to bless us, to enable us to see God, yet we block ourselves from that joy through the unresolved issues within our hearts, all those emotions we keep stuffing down into the depths of our hearts because we either don't want to or can't deal with them.

Many unresolved heart issues block us from experiencing the reality of Jesus' words, "Blessed are the pure in heart." Unforgiveness is a major one. As already noted, the Beatitudes comprise a part of Jesus' Sermon on the Mount, recorded in the Gospel of Matthew. In that sermon, Jesus also gives what we have come to call the Lord's Prayer, in which we pray, "Forgive us our debts, as we also have forgiven our debtors." This is the only part of the prayer on which Jesus further comments. Immediately following the prayer, he adds this teaching: "For if you forgive others their trespasses, your heavenly Father will also forgive you; but if you do not forgive others, neither will your Father forgive your trespasses" (Matt. 6:14-15).

Jesus knew forgiveness was a crucial issue that needed ongoing attention. Not only do we sometimes fail to seek forgiveness for ourselves, but we also hold unforgiveness against someone else. That spirit divides our hearts, hindering us from living fully in the present because our hearts are tied to the past. On Day 1 we asserted that life is a process of moving from birth to the moment in which we will see God; yet if unforgiveness has a hold on our hearts, we can't move toward God because the past has laid claim on us. We are tied to that pain and hurt. Unforgiveness thwarts God's blessing and punishes not the person we refuse to forgive but ourselves. We are the ones who experience the pain and hurt.

"Blessed are the pure in heart." They do not harbor blame and grudges against others. They acknowledge and confess their sin and receive forgiveness.

Reflecting and Recording

Spend a few minutes contemplating emotions you have stuffed deep down in your heart. What anger, unforgiveness, or resentment waits to spill out if you open the door? Make a few notes to get these issues clearly in your mind.

Be specific now. Are you holding a grudge against someone whom you need to forgive? Or is there someone you have wronged from whom you need to ask forgiveness? Name these people here.

Pray now for these persons and for the willingness to forgive. Close your time with prayer, being honest with God about the contents of your heart. Know that God's promise is sure, that God is faithful and just, and that God will cleanse you from every wrong.

During the Day

If possible, contact the persons named above, confess to them, and ask forgiveness. If you prefer to do this through a letter, write it today. Continue praying the petitions of David from the affirmation card or pages 145–46. Pray them three or four times daily.

✠

DAY 5

Single-Mindedness

As we have explored the meaning of having a pure heart, we have focused on an understanding of purity as wholeness, singleness of nature, being undivided at the center of our being. This is important because often we think of purity only in terms of cleanliness. We must be pure and spotless, and with that comes blamelessness.

If we stay focused there, we will miss the full meaning of this Beatitude. Though this Beatitude and the whole of Jesus' teaching stress *inner* cleanness, to be "pure in heart" does not mean to be morally perfect, thus free of every stain of sin. Jesus came to redeem sinners, and he knew that none of us is sinless. This Beatitude, then, has much to do with sincerity, with being *single-minded*.

The epistle of James addresses this issue:

My brothers and sisters, whenever you face trials of any kind, consider it nothing but joy, because you know that the testing of your faith produces endurance; and let endurance have its full effect, so that you may be mature and complete, lacking in nothing.

If any of you is lacking in wisdom, ask God, who gives to all generously and ungrudgingly, and it will be given you. But ask in faith, never doubting, for the one who doubts is like a wave of the sea, driven and tossed by the wind; for the doubter, being double-minded and unstable in every way, must not expect to receive anything from the Lord. (James 1:2-8)

The Greek word translated as "double-minded" is *dipsuchos*; it literally means a person with two souls or two minds. One mind believes; the other disbelieves. Thus the double-minded person becomes a walking civil war in whom trust and distrust of God wage a continual battle.

This is a captivating image—"the double-minded." These persons back away from life or live as though life were a practice game, getting ready or saving themselves for the real thing, which will come later. But the double-minded are like waves on the sea, driven not by their own will but by the will of the wind.

A university freshman was about to go on her first blind date. Her roommate was making all the arrangements and asked whether she preferred Southern or Northern boys. A Midwesterner, the freshman was innocently unaware of such subtle distinctions and asked, "Well, what is the difference?"

Her worldly-wise roommate answered, "Southern boys are more romantic. They will take you walking in the moonlight and whisper sweet nothings in your ear. Northern boys are more active. They like to go places and do exciting things."

The girl pondered the contrast and then asked wistfully, "Could you please find me a Southern boy from as far North as possible?"

Isn't it true? We want to negotiate in the same fashion. We're double-minded. We're like John Bunyan's character, Mr. Facing-Both-Ways.

Some readers will remember the lines from the song that encouraged us to "accentuate the positive" and "eliminate the negative" but especially cautioned, "Don't mess with Mister In-Between." That's more than good upbeat philosophy set to music. It's theology—biblical faith. A long time before this popular song, a singer of Israel discerned God saying, "I hate the double-minded" (Ps. 119:113). Then, in the closing book of the Bible, Revelation, John was instructed to write to the church in Laodicea: "I know your works; you are neither cold nor hot. I wish that you were either cold or hot. So, because you are lukewarm, and neither cold nor hot, I am about to spit you out of my mouth" (Rev. 3:15-16).

This is what James was saying: "For the one who doubts is like a wave of the sea, driven and tossed by the wind; for the doubter, being double-minded and unstable in every way, must not expect to receive anything from the Lord" (vv. 6-8).

Blessed are the single-minded. They are focused and sincere, and the Lord will honor them with his presence.

Reflecting and Recording

Look carefully at the last three or four weeks of your life. List some issues or problems you have dealt with and/or decisions you have made.

Now consider each of these questions: How did the negative and positive war with each other? How did you experience double-mindedness?

■ ■ ■

Write a prayer, confessing your double-mindedness, your temptation to take the easy way, and your desire to trust God but your failure to do so. Include a commitment to be single-minded.

During the Day

If you could not contact the persons you named yesterday, confessing and asking for forgiveness, do so today.

Pay attention to the occasions today when you experience double-mindedness. Don't leave issues or relationships hanging; be single-minded.

Continue using the petitions of David (pp. 145–46). Pray them three or four times today.

DAY 6

Moral Conditions for Spiritual Vision

In his brief, pungent commentary on the sixth Beatitude, New Testament scholar Archibald M. Hunter said, "What does it mean to 'see God'? Since 'no [one] hath ever seen God,' it is not a matter of optics but of spiritual fellowship. It is 'to be near God, and to know him, and to rejoice in him, all in one' (Montefiore). To enjoy such fellowship, says Jesus, a man must be wholly sincere. 'There are moral conditions for spiritual vision.'" (Hunter, *A Pattern for Life*, 39)

To respond to and appropriate the blessing Jesus promised to "the pure in heart," we must stay aware of the simple fact that *we see only what we are able to see*. This is patently and obviously true in the physical realm, and we may think it a bit silly to be reminded. It may not be so obvious in the spiritual realm. Thus, Hunter could claim there are moral conditions for spiritual vision. And William Temple, one-time archbishop of Canterbury, could define purity of heart as "a passionate aspiration towards the holiness of God." (Hunter, *A Pattern for Life*, 39) The epistle of James does not mince words about this dimension of the gospel and the nature of the Christian life.

> What good is it, my brothers and sisters, if you say you have faith but do not have works? Can faith save you? If a brother or sister is naked and lacks daily food, and one of you says to them, "Go in peace; keep warm and eat your fill," and yet you do not supply their bodily needs, what is the good of that? So faith by itself, if it has no works, is dead. (James 2:14-17)

We can't miss the point, which is the point of the entire epistle of James: We must be doers of the Word and not hearers only. How do people ever get the notion that our behavior has no relationship to our spiritual status? If this were true, there would be no difference between the lives of Christians and non-Christians.

Consider this: An article in the *Washington Post*, dated June 21, 2003, says 41 percent of Americans claim to be born again. Barna research in 2004 indicated 38 percent of Americans claim to be born again. Think of that—over one-third of the U.S. population claiming to be born again! If that were true, do you think our nation would be drowning in drugs, wallowing in pornography, allowing millions to go hungry and without shelter, and encouraging self-serving government officials to cut welfare in order to balance a budget that has been unbalanced for years because it gave more attention to the rich than the poor? Do you think we would be in the mess we're in if one-third of us really were Christians, listened to Jesus, and paid attention to James? "If a brother or sister is naked and lacks daily food, and one of you says to them, 'Go in peace; keep warm and eat your fill,' and yet you do not supply their bodily needs, what is the good of that? So faith by itself, if it has no works, is dead."

Do we mock the gospel when we reduce its requirements to simply believing that Christ died for our sins, giving intellectual assent to that truth and accepting by faith the eternal security he offers?

"Blessed are the pure in heart." They know there are moral conditions for spiritual vision. Thus, to be pure in heart, they must passionately aspire for the holiness of God.

Reflecting and Recording

Spend a few minutes reflecting on and examining your life in relation to this claim: Purity of heart is "a passionate aspiration towards the holiness of God."

Now think about the past three months of your life. How well have you done at following James's exhortation "Be doers of the word, and not merely hearers" (1:22)? How would your acquaintances evaluate you in that regard?

■ ■ ■

Think of an occasion when you were a *doer* of the Word and not simply a *hearer*, and an occasion when you were not a doer but a hearer only. Then spend a few minutes in prayer, expressing your desire for purity of heart.

■ ■ ■

During the Day

As you move through this day, remain aware that there must be some way in which you act as a Christian that would not be the same if you were not a Christian.

✠

DAY 7

A Beautiful Impossibility

This is the message we have heard from him and proclaim to you, that God is light and in him there is no darkness at all. If we say that we have fellowship with him while we are walking in darkness, we lie and do not do what is true; but if we walk in the light as he himself is in the light, we have fellowship with one another, and the blood of Jesus his Son cleanses us from all sin. If we say that we have no sin, we deceive ourselves, and the truth is not in us. If we confess our sins, he who is faithful and just will forgive us our sins and cleanse us from all unrighteousness. (1 John 1:5-9)

Someone has described the Beatitudes as "a beautiful impossibility." Unfortunately, if we focus only on the dimension of purity that emphasizes cleanliness, that is exactly what Jesus' words become: a beautiful impossibility. None of us is spotless, blameless, pure. Scripture stresses this fact over and over again. If we say we are pure, if we say we are without sin, we deceive ourselves, and God's truth does not reside within us. So we return to reflecting on the need for honest self-assessment, confession, repentance, and forgiveness as essentials for having a pure heart.

Many issues divide our hearts and impede God's blessing—unresolved anger, lust, greed, and control, to name a few. All of these conditions require radical treatment. God can create pure hearts within us. In fact, God promises to do so. But it's radical business, this transformation that God creates within us.

I will give them one heart, and put a new spirit within them; I will remove the heart of stone from their flesh and give them a heart of flesh, so that they may follow my statutes and keep my ordinances and obey them. Then they shall be my people, and I will be their God. (Ezek. 11:19-20)

Like any surgery, the heart transplant God performs can be painful. Transformation is never easy because it requires that we look honestly within ourselves, examining our own hearts. Not only that, but we have to be honest with God and allow God to peel back the various layers of our hearts to expose the parts we work so hard to keep hidden. And hiding our hearts—shielding them from scrutiny, dividing and compartmentalizing them—is an ability we humans have mastered. We are connoisseurs of deceit, denial, and contradiction, spinning the truth to avoid unmasking the hidden parts of our heart.

In one of his sermons at Ginghamsburg United Methodist Church, Mike Slaughter told the story of a friend who in his thirties discovered he had a cancerous tumor in the middle of his brain. All the doctors told him that nothing could be done, that he needed to get his affairs in order because he was going to die. He didn't accept that diagnosis and began searching for a doctor who would take the risk to save him. He flew all over the country searching and finally found a doctor willing to undertake the necessary radical surgery. This doctor removed the man's tumor, and the rest of the cancer was eradicated through radiation. Mike's friend lived another ten years after this surgery, finally dying of an unrelated cause.

Cancer is a disease where unhealthy cells overwhelm healthy ones. Unhealthy cells and healthy cells are always at odds with each other, battling until the unhealthy cells overcome the healthy cells, consuming them. Cancer requires radical treatment. The transformation necessary for us to receive pure hearts is equally radical. Mike Slaughter says that transformation is not simply a "spiritual cosmic hug" (Slaughter, "Journey of the Heart: Inside Stuff," sermon preached at Ginghamsburg United Methodist Church, February 16–17, 2002). Many of us seek out churches hoping to receive "spiritual hugs" that will resolve all our issues. But pure hearts require more than just spiritual hugs; they also require radical transformation. Such transformation requires a cross.

To know that "God so loved the world that he gave his only Son" is different from knowing that God loves *me* so much that he gave his only Son. It is not enough to know with my mind that God forgives *our* sins; I must experience God's forgiveness of *my* sins.

Acknowledging ourselves as sinners and becoming personally aware of God's forgiveness is the central event that makes us Christians. Paul described it this way: "We are ruled by the love of Christ, now that we recognize that one man died for everyone, which means that they all share in his death. He died for all so that those who live should no longer live for themselves, but only for him who died and was raised to life for their sake" (2 Cor. 5:14-15, GNT). This is not a halfway sort of event. God doesn't do things partially.

Some of us may need radical treatment. We must get honest with God, emptying out our closets in order to allow God, who is faithful and just, to forgive our sins and cleanse us of every wrong.

Blessed are the pure in heart, for they hide nothing; they are willing to allow the radical transformation that comes through the unconditional love and forgiveness our Lord provides.

Reflecting and Recording

Spend a few minutes reflecting on the following claims:

We are connoisseurs of deceit, denial, and contradiction, spinning the truth to avoid unmasking the hidden parts of our hearts.

■ ■ ■

Pure hearts require more than spiritual hugs; they also require radical transformation, . . . a cross.

■ ■ ■

It is not enough to know with my mind that God forgives *our* sins; I must experience God's forgiveness of *my* sins.

■ ■ ■

If you are in a group sharing this workbook, you will meet today. Glance through this week's content and make notes of questions or issues you'd like to discuss.

During the Day

Guard yourself against the tendency to cram emotions deep into your heart where no one can see. Be aware of opportunities to be honest with God and others regarding your heart issues. Continue to pray the petitions of David (see pp. 145–46 or use the affirmation card).

✠

Group Meeting
for Week Six

Leader: You will need a whiteboard or newsprint for this session.

Sharing Together

You are approaching the end of this workbook venture. Only two more sessions remain, so your group may want to discuss its future. Would the group like to stay together for a longer time? Are there resources (books, tapes, periodicals) the group would like to use corporately? This workbook is a sequel to our previous one, *The Workbook on the Ten Commandments.* If you have not already used that resource, you may want to consider doing so. If all group members attend the same church, think about ways to share this workbook study with others.

1.   Invite the group to read together the following verse from Charles Wesley's hymn "O for a Heart to Praise My God."

> O for a heart to praise my God,
> a heart from sin set free,
> a heart that always feels thy blood so freely shed for me.

Ask a volunteer to offer a prayer for this session.

2.   Invite two or three persons to share some fresh insight they received from the workbook this week.

3.   Invite anyone who will to share particular questions or difficulties with the workbook this week. Don't rush; take enough time for the group to respond.

4.   "The heart of the matter is always a matter of the heart." In light of this claim and the responses just shared, spend ten to twelve minutes discussing the following assertions:

• The heart determines our character.
• The heart is the center of our emotions.
• The heart influences our will.
• The heart is the seat of our moral integrity.

5.   *Leader:* Write on whiteboard or newsprint these column headings:

Clean Hands   Pure Heart

Invite group members to call out words or phrases that describe clean hands and pure hearts. Refer to Reflecting and Recording on Day 2.

6. In light of this listing, spend eight to ten minutes discussing what it means for our heart and hands to be clean . . . pure . . . undivided. Which is the most common? the most difficult?

7. Invite someone to read Psalm 51:11-12 aloud as a prayer.

8. Invite someone to read two paragraphs from Day 4 (pp. 145–46), beginning with "Many unresolved heart issues. . . ." Then spend eight to ten minutes discussing our need for forgiveness and the fact that we must be forgiving in order to be forgiven.

9. Ask for a volunteer to read the last two paragraphs before Reflecting and Recording in Day 6, beginning with "Do we mock the gospel. . . ." Then spend six to eight minutes discussing the need for our faith to be reflected in our works.

10. Spend the rest of your time addressing group members' questions or issues that have been raised by the consideration of this Beatitude.

Praying Together

One simple guide for prayer is an acronym: ACTS (A = adoration; C = confession; T = thanksgiving; S = supplication [intercession on behalf of others and expressions of earnest desire for God's will in our lives and the world]).

It is usually easy in a corporate setting to offer prayers of adoration, thanksgiving, and even supplication. But corporate confession—naming our personal and corporate sins aloud in the presence of others—doesn't come easily.

Hopefully, by now you feel "safe" and "at home" in this group and can begin to be more honest and risk more intimate sharing.

1. Ask for a volunteer to offer a prayer of adoration and thanksgiving. In adoration, we praise God for who God is; in thanksgiving, we thank God for what God has done.

2. Now enter a time of confession. Begin with a time of silence, with the leader guiding in a fashion such as this:

    > In silence now, let us make our individual confessions as we consider the condition of our hearts. Do you have a hard heart? *(Pause after each question for silent reflection.)*
    > Are you hiding something from a loved one?
    > Have you been deliberately deceitful this past week?
    > Have you lied? cheated?
    > Have you lusted? given attention to pornography?
    > What about sins of omission—failure to be merciful?
    > Spend another minute now examining your heart and your hands. Do you have clean hands and a pure heart?

3. *Leader:* Offer a brief, verbal prayer, seeking to express earnest confession. Then invite the group to join you in this corporate prayer:

Merciful God,
we confess that we have not loved you with our whole heart.
We have failed to be an obedient church.
We have not done your will,
we have broken your law,
we have rebelled against your love,
we have not loved our neighbors,
and we have not heard the cry of the needy.
Forgive us, we pray.
Free us for joyful obedience,
through Jesus Christ our Lord.
Amen.
("A Service of Word and Table I," *The United Methodist Hymnal*, 8)

4.   Invite a volunteer to close with a prayer of supplication—earnestly praying for the forgiveness of sins, for healing and wholeness, and for God's will to be done in our lives and in the world.

Week Seven

The Peacemakers

✠

DAY 1

Butt Out!

Blessed are the peacemakers, for they will be called children of God. (Matt. 5:9)

As adults, we understand that our world is not a peaceful place. A significant transition to adulthood involves recognizing that the world is not the safe haven most parents have been able to create for their children but is, in reality, a dangerous and strife-filled place. Jesus was all too aware of that reality. He understood the fallen nature of humanity. He recognized the power of evil and the destruction that emanates from it. That's why he taught us to love our enemies and pray for those who persecute us. Only then, he said, will we be acting as true children of God (Matt. 5:44-45). Because Jesus understood how prone we are to conflict and violence, he defined the life his followers were to lead in sharp contrast to the rest of the world, challenging us:

> If you love those who love you, what reward do you have? Do not even the tax collectors do the same? And if you greet only your brothers and sisters, what more are you doing than others? Do not even the Gentiles do the same? (Matt. 5:46-47)

Jesus knew how badly our world needs peacemakers. That's why he proclaimed that God blesses those who work for peace and why he promised that the peacemakers would be called children of God.

The Greek word for *peace* is *eirene*; the Greek word for *peacemakers* is *eirenopoios*. Scholars remind us that the latter word should be taken in its active sense of peacemakers, not peacekeepers or peace lovers. It is the peacemakers—those who actively seek peace, always working for reconciliation—who are blessed.

The Hebrew word for peace, *shalom*, never describes only an inactive state or the absence of trouble. It means wholeness, everything that works toward our highest good. The peacemaker is one who continually expresses active goodwill. Such a person does not evade issues that bring tension and division but recognizes them, names them, and deals with them so that reconciliation and peace may reign.

The gospel message is clear. Paul also reiterates Jesus' demand for our lives:

> Do not repay anyone evil for evil, but take thought for what is noble in the sight of all. If it is possible, so far as it depends on you, live peaceably with all. Beloved, never avenge yourselves, but leave room for the wrath of God; for it is written, "Vengeance is mine, I will repay, says the Lord." No, "if your enemies are hungry, feed them; if they are thirsty, give them something to drink; for by doing this you will heap burning coals on their heads." Do not be overcome by evil, but overcome evil with good. (Rom. 12:17-21)

The message of the New Testament stands in dramatic contrast to the widespread assumptions of our world, a place where violence is so common that it is embedded even in children's video games. James Harnish, an outstanding preacher and writer, once told a story about the capital punishment debate in the California legislature. Apparently Mother Teresa called the governor to suggest that he do what Jesus would do. When a newspaper learned of Mother Teresa's call, it carried an editorial headline blaring, "Mother Teresa, Butt Out!" (Harnish, *Journey to the Center of the Faith*, 117)

As Christians, we like to think of ourselves as peacemakers. We are the ones who will receive the blessing Jesus reserves for peacemakers. Unfortunately, a distinct problem for us in claiming that blessing with integrity is the fact that more often than not, when it comes to Jesus' call to peace and nonviolence, we have found polite ways of telling him to "butt out." The sad reality is that the church has substantially watered down the call of Jesus in our lives. We have neutralized Jesus' demand that we be peacemakers. We have subtly pushed the gospel call for peacemaking and nonviolence into the spiritual realm, with the result that we never actually expect peace to become a reality in our human experience.

Reflecting and Recording

To begin to think concretely about the need for peacemakers, examine the five spheres of life designated below and on the next page. Reflect on each area, and, using single words, phrases, or sentences, name and describe the tensions and conflicts in these areas.

Inner-personal (conflict with yourself)

Family

Community

Nation

World

Pray the prayer attributed to Saint Francis from the affirmation card or pages 53–54.

During the Day

Look at what you recorded about conflict and tension in your family and/or community. Perform at least one peacemaking act today.

DAY 2

Inner-Personal and Interpersonal Conflict

As God's chosen ones, holy and beloved, clothe yourselves with compassion, kindness, humility, meekness, and patience. Bear with one another and, if anyone has a complaint against another, forgive each other; just as the Lord has forgiven you, so you also must forgive. Above all, clothe yourselves with love, which binds everything together in perfect harmony. And let the peace of Christ rule in your hearts, to which indeed you were called in the one body. And be thankful. Let the word of Christ dwell in you richly; teach and admonish one another in all wisdom; and with gratitude in your hearts sing psalms, hymns, and spiritual songs to God. And whatever you do, in word or deed, do everything in the name of the Lord Jesus, giving thanks to God the Father through him. (Col. 3:12-17)

We closed yesterday's reading with this sentence: We have subtly pushed the gospel call for peacemaking and nonviolence into the spiritual realm, with the result that we never actually expect peace to become a reality in our human experience. This notion needs further consideration.

The issue of peace *is* a spiritual matter but not just a *private* spiritual matter. Yet there is a sense in which peace and peacemaking must begin within.

We remember a *Brother Juniper* cartoon, created by Father Justin McCarthy. Brother Juniper, a monk, is visiting the zoo with two young boys. They are looking at a caged bird. The bird, a crowlike creature, looks bedraggled, scantily feathered, and downcast in every way. The label on the bird's cage reads, "Bird of Paradise." Looking at the sign, Brother Juniper comments, "I don't think he quite made it."

That's us, isn't it? Like the bird of paradise, we didn't quite make it. We began our days in Eden, the image of God within us; but somehow along the way, as again and again we turn from God, that image dims. The wholeness of our created being becomes fragmented and divided. As we struggle with God and ourselves, our lives become marked with inner and outer conflicts and a deep sense of restlessness we can't seem to escape.

So, though peacemaking is not only a private spiritual issue, this Beatitude addresses the matter of making peace in our own heart and soul, to still the restlessness, to ease the inner conflict. To some degree, each of us is a walking civil war. Good and evil battle within us. Our commitments pull us in different directions all at once.

There are many reasons for our inner conflict, but much of it arises from the gap between our values and our actions. We hold certain values we have either chosen or accepted from our culture and faith communities. When our actions are out of sync with those values, we feel guilty and conflicted. Fortunately, this kind of inner conflict can be resolved. We can change our behavior or values in order to close the gap. But unfortunately, we are plagued by a deeper problem than a simple conflict between values and action. The gnawing restlessness of our souls, our nagging sense of discontent, stems not from a gap between values and action but a gap between the reality of the world and the yearnings of our souls. The world lays claim on us, convincing us of the importance of science, success, power, and material wealth; yet our souls long for something more. We experience inner conflict as our souls battle between their own true intuition and the false suggestions of the world.

We believe a connection exists between our sense of inner conflict and interpersonal tension and conflict. *The New Yorker* carried a cartoon depicting a common mood: the frame shows a large city library. On the wall is a sign declaring, "Shut the hell up!" A man passing by comments to his wife, "Everybody's on edge these days."

How true of our times. We are all uptight and tense, on edge and stressed out. As our children and grandchildren would say, we badly need to "chill." This need to chill reflects our inner-personal conflict, but it is also played out in interpersonal conflict and estrangement. We will never experience peace in our relationships until we experience it within ourselves.

A contemporary phenomenon that demonstrates the connection between inner- and interpersonal tension and conflict is "road rage." Road rage expresses itself through tailgating, cutting people off, or in extreme cases, shooting someone while competing for position in heavy traffic.

There is no question: we need inner peace. At minimum we need to commit to a working peace treaty as we give ourselves wholly to God. Paul admonishes us, "Let the peace of Christ rule in your hearts" (Col. 3:15).

Reflecting and Recording

Yesterday you named and described your *inner*-personal conflict. Would you describe that as a civil war? Spend some time in self-examination. Do your inner-personal conflicts concern tension between your values and your actions? your faith and your lifestyle?

■ ■ ■

You were also asked yesterday to think about conflict and/or tension in your family. Look back at the notes you wrote about that, and consider whether the interpersonal conflict and/or tension in the family might be caused by inner-personal conflict within a person or persons in the family.

■ ■ ■

Spend the balance of your time reflecting on this question: What kind of peace do I most need?

■ ■ ■

During the Day

Engage someone today in conversation about inner-personal and interpersonal conflict and the possible connection between the two.

As you track the news in various media sources, notice areas where peace is needed.

✠

DAY 3

Reaping Olives from Fig Trees

Does a spring of water bubble out with both fresh water and bitter water? Can you pick olives from a fig tree or figs from a grapevine? No, and you can't draw fresh water from a salty pool.

If you are wise and understand God's ways, live a life of steady goodness so that only good deeds will pour forth. (James 3:11-13, NLT)

We live in difficult times, when terrorists attack with devastating results; when virtually every nation can bring about horrific destruction; when it seems that the only way to bring peace is through using a force strong enough to wipe out perpetrators of violence. As logical as that reasoning may appear, it goes against the gospel witness. James reminds us of nature's order: you can't pick olives from a fig tree or figs from a grapevine or draw fresh water from a salty pool. The same is true of peace and violence. If we want to reap peace, we must plant seeds of peace. If we plant violence, we will surely reap more violence. Claiming Jesus' promise of blessing for peacemakers, then, requires us to be as concerned about means as ends.

As we write this, we mourn the death of a dear friend, Boris Trajkovski, president of the Republic of Macedonia, who was killed in a tragic plane crash in February 2004. As a Methodist lay pastor, Boris understood that the peace God intends for our world is impossible simply through human means. We reap what we sow, and all too often, we sow violence. As he labored to resolve the ethnic struggles in his war-torn country, Boris made no attempt to hide his belief that humans can only *control conflict*, not bring peace. Only the power of Jesus Christ can bring peace. He recognized that even as God used him to provide a light in the darkness of conflict, his role as a secular leader required him to make decisions that went against his faith. He knew that because some of his decisions required violence, peace would not be the result, only the *containment of conflict*. So deep was his conviction that violence is not a means to peace, that when he spoke to an international gathering of Methodists in Oslo, Norway, he asked forgiveness from his brothers and sisters in Christ, proclaiming that Christ is the only means of peace for our world.

If we are to be peacemakers who follow Christ's example, we must guard against a spirit of vengeance in response to the evil we experience. If we succumb to that spirit, evil wins out. If the violence we experience and are exposed to makes us more violent or meaner or less compassionate, the powers of hell will have been victorious. In Romans 12:21 Paul urges us to overcome evil with good. Doing this is difficult enough; but it is impossible to overcome evil with more evil.

This is a difficult word for Americans to hear, particularly after our national experience on September 11, 2001, and the ensuing war in Iraq. Many times during the last several years it has seemed appropriate to many persons to respond to current events with violence, even preemptive violence. Unfortunately, as humans we are too flawed to bring about peace through our own efforts, particularly violent ones. Our endeavors are all too often tainted by greed, arrogance, ignorance, and questionable motives. Only Christ can truly provide our world with the peace it so badly needs. And violence, especially when it is preemptive, stands contrary to the witness of Jesus. Martin Luther King Jr. expressed that truth eloquently in his 1967 Christmas Sermon on Peace:

> We will never have peace in the world until men everywhere recognize that ends are not cut off from means, because the means represent the ideal in the making, and the end in process, and ultimately you can't reach good ends through evil means, because the means represent the seed and the end represents the tree. (King, "Christmas Sermon on Peace," *A Testament of Hope*, ed. James Melvin Washington, 255)

We are called to be peacemakers, not by overcoming evil with more evil but by overcoming it with good.

Reflecting and Recording

Return to Day 1 of this week, page 162, and read the Romans passage. Reflect on the conflicting dynamics of overcoming evil with evil versus overcoming evil with good.

■ ■ ■

When have you sought to overcome some wrong done to you or to a loved one by seeking to repay or avenge the act? Make some notes here about that experience.

When have you responded with forgiveness and love to some wrong done to you or someone you loved—seeking not to repay or avenge but to overcome evil with good? Make some notes about that experience.

In light of your experience and reflections, spend the rest of your time thinking about this question: How possible is it to live Jesus' way and return evil with good?

■ ■ ■

During the Day

Talk with someone today about an obvious evil in your community—an area of conflict and tension—asking, "What needs to happen for peace to be brought to this situation?"

Pray the following prayer continually today and in the coming days:

Lord, make me an instrument of your peace.

✠

DAY 4

Communities of Light

Once you were darkness, but now in the Lord you are light. Live as children of light—for the fruit of the light is found in all that is good and right and true. Try to find out what is pleasing to the Lord. Take no part in the unfruitful works of darkness, but instead expose them. (Eph. 5:8-11)

There have been many descriptions of Jesus' way of nonviolence, the Christian call to peacemaking. Martin Luther King Jr. lived out a philosophy of nonviolent resistance that he claimed through the influence of Mahatma Gandhi. E. Stanley Jones, a renowned evangelist, writer, and missionary to India who influenced Gandhi and was influenced by him, demonstrated commitment to the gospel of "unquenchable good will, the law of love in human relationships." The Quakers coined the phrase "Christian pacifism."

Regardless of the descriptive words you use, a common denominator is Jesus' outlining of a radical alternative to violence. An unexpected consequence of our attempts to describe this radical alternative is the fact that we frequently return to the word *pacifism*, which unfortunately sounds a lot like the word *passive*. Unlike pacifism, passivity doesn't challenge our tendency to accommodate Jesus into our own worldviews rather than being transformed into his way of life. Thus, we live in the passive comfort of our spiritual interpretation of Jesus' call, believing that the peace for which he calls us to work will never be realized this side of the kingdom.

Such passivity stands in dramatic opposition to the life to which Jesus has called us. It places us outside Jesus' promised blessing to peacemakers. Working for peace is never a passive operation. To follow Jesus is never to react passively in the face of injustice, abuse, or undeserved suffering. Being a peacemaker who follows the way of Jesus is always an energetic and risky endeavor, filled with vigorous, complicated, costly, and insistent goodwill. If we follow Jesus with integrity, we liberate the oppressed and set the captives free. We not only seek justice but *do* justice and work to transform brokenness into wholeness in all areas of life. In proclaiming our loyalty to the one who "descended to the dead" (Apostles' Creed), we willingly descend into places of violence and death in order to bring healing and life. Though the peacemaking of Jesus is indeed a risky endeavor, it is also one with tremendous promised blessing.

On the Sunday after 9/11, Mike Slaughter provided a wonderful metaphor for the reality of our time and the life to which Jesus calls us:

> From 1939 to 1944 Hitler and the evil force of the Nazi empire were invading sovereign states with little resistance. But there was an operation being planned under the code name Operation Overlord. Supreme commander over its execution was General Dwight D. Eisenhower. Preparation for the invasion began months before the actual event. At 12:15 AM on June 6, 1944, the massive invasion began. The U.S. forces established two beachheads on the coast of Normandy—Utah Beach and Omaha Beach. Omaha Beach was the scene of the fiercest fighting. Because of the heroic efforts of D-Day, the days of the evil Nazi empire were numbered.
>
> Evil has had its plan on planet Earth since Cain murdered his brother, Abel. It has slithered and hissed its way with little formidable opposition through the millennia. But there was a cosmic operation being planned under the code name Lion of Judah. Supreme commander over its execution was Jesus of Nazareth, Prince of Peace. In the early hours of the morning approximately two thousand years ago in a Middle Eastern community named Bethlehem, the armies of heaven invaded planet Earth and established beachhead communities of light. These communities have continued to be the scenes of the fiercest fighting, but the true Light has come into the world, and darkness can never put it out. (Slaughter, "I Will Fear No Evil," sermon, September 15–16, 2001)

Paul called us to "live as children of light" and to "take no part in the unfruitful works of darkness." To inherit Jesus' blessing, we must abandon passivity and actively live out our faith as beachhead communities of light. We must claim God's promise of victory—not through force but through the cross. Jesus undertook the amazing risk of the cross, abandoning the ease of his life of teaching and healing and submitting himself to the terror of evil, thus providing a victory that stands in complete contrast to the world.

When Israel went into battle at night, men stood watch on the front line, placing themselves between the enemy and Israel's troops. The night Jesus was arrested, he asked his disciples to watch and pray while he prayed. When we say yes to Jesus, we become watchfolk. We actively put ourselves on the front line for the life of the world. We become radical agents of love, actively working for God's reign of peace to become a reality in our world, committing our lives to the invasion of light and love for the ultimate defeat of death, knowing all the while that the victory has been won and we will be blessed.

Reflecting and Recording

On Day 1, you made notes about tension and conflicts in your community, in the nation, and in the world. Review those notes and add to them if something comes to mind.

Focus now on your community. Does your congregation seek to be a community of light in response to conflict and tension? Spend time reflecting on what you personally might do to be a peacemaker in your community. What might you do to challenge your congregation and/or Christian friends to act as peacemakers in your community?

■ ■ ■

During the Day

Continue to use the prayer "Lord, make me an instrument of your peace" as you move throughout the day. Use some common happenings to call you to that prayer: the ringing of the telephone, stopping at a traffic light, media announcements of conflict and violence. Incorporate this prayer into your mealtime blessings.

DAY 5

To Be Like Jesus

In Christ Jesus you are all children of God through faith. As many of you as were baptized into Christ have clothed yourselves with Christ. There is no longer Jew or Greek, there is no longer slave or free, there is no longer male and female; for all of you are one in Christ Jesus. And if you belong to Christ, then you are Abraham's offspring, heirs according to the promise. (Gal. 3:26-29)

Our world is addicted to violent power. Over and over throughout history, violence has been the preferred means of problem solving. As Christians we believe that even at its best, the world is a fallen place. Thus, we shouldn't be surprised by the brokenness, the tendency toward violence, and the way God gets pushed to the sidelines of consciousness or even forsaken altogether. In fact, as we have noted, there are many times in which a violent response seems to make sense, given the wickedness of our world. Yet the cross stands as a radical departure from the way of the world. Jesus' self-giving love, poured out for us on the cross, provides an extreme alternative to violence as a response to evil. It is a response the world has a great deal of trouble understanding, but it is the only response if the world desires redemption.

Webster's 11th New Collegiate Dictionary defines Christian as "manifesting the qualities or spirit of Christ." According to the *Encarta Dictionary*, a Christian is "a believer in Jesus Christ as savior . . . [one] who tries to follow his teachings and example." Both definitions target what Paul pointed out to the Galatians in the passage that opened today's reading: When Christ dwells in our hearts through faith, we become like Jesus—we receive "Jesus DNA" that overrides all other genetic codes such as gender or race. When Jesus promises that peacemakers will be blessed and called children of God, he clearly signals an important trait that stems from Jesus DNA: a commitment to peace. When we make a commitment to peace, to Christian nonviolence, we live from our Jesus DNA; we show the world what children of God look like. Simply put, Christian peacemaking flows from a deep-seated yearning to be like Jesus, a desire to let our Jesus DNA become the dominant force in our lives, enabling us to experience and base our lives on Jesus' love, follow his commandments faithfully, and bring our behavior into harmony with his vision of the kingdom.

This is intrinsic to the Beatitude "Blessed are the peacemakers, for they will be called children of God." Again there are connections between these principles of the kingdom. The sixth Beatitude says the pure in heart will *see* God; this seventh Beatitude says they will be called children of God. We are blessed when we try to make peace, because we are doing Godlike work. We are living as children who have inherited traits of their parents. It is God's nature to make peace. God's Son, Jesus, was called the Prince of Peace. As Christians, we not only *become* like Jesus, we *act* like Jesus. That means we are to be peacemakers.

The cross grounds this desire to be like Jesus. Paul understood both the centrality of the cross and its seeming absurdity from the perspective of the world:

> I know very well how foolish the message of the cross sounds to those who are on the road to destruction. But we who are being saved recognize this message as the very power of God. . . . God's way seems foolish to the Jews because they want a sign from heaven to prove it is true. And it is foolish to the Greeks because they believe only what agrees with their own wisdom. So when we preach that Christ was crucified, the Jews are offended, and the Gentiles say it's all nonsense. But to those called by God to salvation,

both Jews and Gentiles, Christ is the mighty power of God and the wonderful wisdom of God. This "foolish" plan of God is far wiser than the wisest of human plans, and God's weakness is far stronger than the greatest of human strength. (1 Cor. 1:18, 22-25, NLT)

As we write this commentary, Mel Gibson's movie *The Passion of the Christ* stands at the center of media controversy. The controversy illustrates the relevance of scripture for our times. Paul's word about the cross being foolishness rings uniquely true, given the media's continual focus on the possibility of anti-Semitic interpretations and whether or not the story is "accurate" rather than on Jesus' sacrificial love and willingness to give his life for the world. Regardless of our opinion of Mel Gibson's *Passion* (it is, after all, nothing more than a depiction of one man's vision of Jesus' sacrifice), the film is not God's own definitive revelation, yet it does provide us with a stark look at Jesus' way of redemptive suffering. It illustrates, in painfully graphic ways, a self-giving love that undercuts the assumptions of power in our world. As difficult as it may be for us to comprehend, the cross of Jesus Christ is the definitive characteristic of the way God chooses to be in relationship with us. The way of redemptive suffering, the way of self-giving love, the way of self-sacrifice and nonviolence—that is the way of Jesus. That is what is contained in the cross. Living out of our Jesus DNA, then, requires that we take up our own cross and follow him.

As we suggested on Day 2, if we are to obtain the blessing Jesus promises peacemakers, we must begin with ourselves. We must personally claim the redemption offered through Jesus' suffering. After all, while we see the horrific power of violence in the Cross, we also know the conquering power of suffering love in the Resurrection. We become peacemakers first by dealing with the places deep within us where we wrestle with anger, resentment, hostility, and other negative and destructive emotions. It is impossible to bear witness to peacemaking if our own souls are entangled in animosity. As peacemakers, we claim for ourselves the victorious power of Jesus' suffering love and the healing and redemption it affords us. In nurturing our relationship with Christ, we gain an inner peace that emanates outward in a commitment to peacemaking, a commitment that shows the failure not of God but of violence.

Reflecting and Recording

Spend some time pondering this statement: We become peacemakers first by dealing with the places deep within us where we wrestle with anger, resentment, hostility, and other negative and destructive emotions.

■ ■ ■

Read again the notes you made on Day 1 about inner-personal tension and conflict. How do you deal with your inner self? How often do you claim the victorious power of Jesus' suffering love and the redemption it affords?

■ ■ ■

What persons or groups in your community would you describe as peacemakers? Make some notes about them here.

Is the way of the cross—the way of self-giving love, nonviolence, or self-sacrifice—a part of the work of peace the persons you named above are performing? If not, how could "the way of the cross" add to their effectiveness?

During the Day

Call or write someone you know who works for peace in some situation, expressing your appreciation. Ask him or her how you can help.

DAY 6

No Blameless Victims

Now in Christ Jesus you who once were far off have been brought near by the blood of Christ. For he is our peace; in his flesh he has made both groups into one and has broken down the dividing wall, that is, the hostility between us. He has abolished the law with its commandments and ordinances, that he might create in himself one new humanity in place of the two, thus making peace, and might reconcile both groups to God in one body through the cross, thus putting to death that hostility through it. (Eph. 2:13-16)

For most of this week, we have focused on our role as peacemakers in the context of a world wracked by violence. We noted on Day 2 that inner-personal and interpersonal peace are issues we must consider. Let's focus now on our responsibility to be peacemakers in the context of our individual sphere of relationships. Like our larger world, human relationships often lack peace. Among other things, we struggle with conflict, estrangement, anger, bitterness, unforgiveness, misunderstanding, and alienation. Yet these are not the experiences God intends for us in relationship with other human beings. God desires that we be reconciled with each other, even as we are reconciled with God. As we read in the above passage from Ephesians, Christ has broken down all walls of hostility so that we can have peace with one another.

As Christians we affirm that Christ has broken down walls of hostility between human beings, even though our human experience points to a continued lack of peace with one another. This disconnection provides evidence of our need to commit ourselves to peacemaking after the example of Christ. Peacemaking, particularly in individual human relationships, is intimately connected to forgiveness and reconciliation. We cannot experience peace without reconciling ourselves to God and to others. This truth is as frustratingly obvious as achieving it is painfully difficult. Reconciliation and the peace it affords are difficult for every human being, because not all of the other human beings who inhabit the world and our lives (including ourselves) are easy to get along with.

Numerous blocks exist to reconciliation; however, we would like to highlight one in particular: the very way in which we distinguish our conflicts—around the framework of oppression and liberation. While space does not allow an in-depth discussion of this framework, suffice it to say that when conflict arises within individual relationships or between groups, there are always at least two opposing parties: the oppressed (victims) and the oppressors (perpetrators). Our natural inclination is to claim the higher moral ground of victim, in contrast to the other party whom we cast as the perpetrator because we believe they have wronged us in some way. Because humans have a predisposition to perceive themselves as victim rather than perpetrator, each of us claims the mantle of victim engaged against another in a struggle for liberation.

The categories of oppressed and oppressor do not need to be abandoned completely. To do so would be an affront to the millions of people who have suffered at the hands of violent oppressors—battered women, persecuted minorities, tortured dissidents, exploited slaves. Yet these categories are flawed inasmuch as they arm us for battle rather than prepare us for reconciliation. In addition, they seldom take into account the messiness of conflict. Human conflict is never cut-and-dried. It is never as simple as pure wickedness butting heads with irrefutable good. On the contrary, scripture attests to the reality that often people are oppressed, "everyone by another and everyone by a neighbor" (Isa. 3:5). Conflicts are made up of the messy, knotted histories of individuals and groups, where extracting the innocent from the culpable proves almost impossible because seldom are there blameless victims.

Finally, the oppression/liberation framework hinders rather than helps the cause of reconciliation and peace inasmuch as it provides no framework for relationship in the event our battle is won. How are we to relate to the person or group who has wronged us after we defeat them in this battle of victim versus perpetrator? When the liberated oppressed achieve victory, how do they live alongside their conquered oppressors? In his book *Exclusion and Embrace*, Miroslav Volf rightly observes that "liberators are known for not taking off their soldiers' uniforms." Zygmunt Bauman expands that thought:

> As history progresses, injustice tends to be compensated for by injustice-with-role-reversal. It is only the victors, as long as their victory stays unchallenged, who mistake, or misrepresent, that compensation as the triumph of justice. Superior morality is all too often the morality of the superior. (Bauman, *Life in Fragments: Essays in Postmodern Morality*, 183f., as quoted in Volf, *Exclusion and Embrace*, 104)

Ultimately, if we are to be peacemakers and thus claim Jesus' promise in the Beatitudes, we must abandon the oppression/liberation system and find a new overarching framework for our conflict resolution, even as we recognize the value of the individual categories of oppressed and oppressor. Some might be uncomfortable abandoning this system, seeing reconciliation as important but only after justice is done and liberation and freedom achieved. How can we reconcile with the one who has wronged us unless we first experience liberation from the pain he or she has caused? How can we reconcile with the one who has wronged us unless he or she is first brought to justice? While those are significant questions, we believe a better question is the one posed by Miroslav Volf: "Will justice ever be done if the ultimate goal is not reconciliation?" (Volf, *Exclusion and Embrace*, 105)

We believe that love is the ultimate value we must strive for as we seek to bring peace to our relationships. After all, love lay at the heart of Christ's self-giving sacrifice on the cross. Love grounded Jesus' suffering on the cross, through which he shared in his own body and soul all the sufferings of the poor and weak and at the same time offered a sacrificial gift of forgiveness to the guilty. Any who have suffered through conflict in relationships can find comfort in the crucified Christ—who was oppressed and afflicted but didn't open his mouth (Isa. 53:7). However, as we seek peace through reconciliation, we must also be mindful of Paul's word to the Romans that Christ "died for the ungodly." We must remember that in one act—the Cross—Jesus stands in solidarity with all victims and at the same time offers forgiveness and atonement to all perpetrators. If we desire peace, we can gain it in part through the comfort Christ offers through his suffering on the cross. But that peace will not be fully realized until we also follow his example of forgiveness for the guilty.

Reflecting and Recording

Can you recall an experience of conflict when you felt you were the victim, yet the person who wronged you thought himself or herself the victim? Make some notes to get the experience fully in mind.

What is the clearest demonstration you know of reconciliation not working because the persons involved perceived themselves as victims and others as perpetrators?

■ ■ ■

Spend some time pondering this question: Will justice ever be done if the ultimate goal is not reconciliation?

■ ■ ■

Now reflect on this claim: In one act—the Cross—Jesus stands in solidarity with all victims and at the same time offers forgiveness and atonement to all perpetrators.

During the Day

Notice news reports of tension and conflict. How often do you observe the victim/perpetrator, oppressor/liberator motif at work?

Engage someone in conversation about this notion. If possible, talk to a person who feels he or she belongs to an oppressed group. Ask what this person thinks about the question Will justice ever be accomplished if the ultimate goal is not reconciliation?

DAY 7

The Peace of Embrace

> When you are offering your gift at the altar, if you remember that your brother or sister has something against you, leave your gift there before the altar and go; first be reconciled to your brother or sister, and then come and offer your gift. (Matt. 5:23-24)

The Greek language has three words for love: *eros*, *philia*, and *agape*. *Eros* is what we think of as romantic love. *Philia* is the reciprocal love between friends. *Agape*, however, is greater and more powerful than either *eros* or *philia*. Martin Luther King Jr. described agape as "understanding, creative, redemptive good will for all [humans]." (King, "The Power of Nonviolence," in *A Testament of Hope*, 13) Agape is not weak or passive; rather, it is active. It not only seeks the reconciliation of individuals but also works to create and preserve community.

Yesterday we mentioned the need for peacemaking, as well as the difficulty in achieving it, in our relationships. We focused on our need for reconciliation and beginning that process by recognizing that in the cross Christ offers solidarity with victims and all who suffer—and at the same time offers forgiveness and atonement to perpetrators and all who are guilty. Only through understanding Christ's love for both sides of our conflicts will we be able to take the steps needed for reconciliation and the peace it affords. Agape love must be the foundation of our movement toward reconciliation. It must motivate us to go to any length to restore community; it must soften our hearts so that we are willing to forgive, not seven times but seventy times seven, in order to restore community. It must give us the courage to leave our places of worship and seek out those we have wronged in order to restore community.

But how do we offer agape love? Miroslav Volf describes a wonderful metaphor for the process of reconciliation and peacemaking: embrace—not so much a physical embrace but the "dynamic relationship between the self and the other that embrace symbolizes and enacts." (Volf, *Exclusion and Embrace*, 141) Volf outlines four essential elements for embrace to occur: (1) opening the arms, (2) waiting, (3) closing the arms, and (4) opening them again. The continuity of these elements is important. If we stop after opening our arms and waiting, embrace will not occur. If we stop after closing our arms, then rather than creating embrace we will have created a situation of force and oppression. Thus, all four elements, integrated into one movement, are necessary.

The first element, opening our arms, signals that we are reaching for another. My open arms indicate both that I have made space within myself for you and that I have moved outside myself toward you. In opening our arms we offer a gesture of invitation:

> Like a door left open for an expected friend, they [open arms] are a call to come in. No knock is necessary, no question on the part of the other whether she can come in is needed, just the announcement of arrival and stepping over the threshold. (Volf, *Exclusion and Embrace*, 142)

In addition to being an invitation, open arms are also a soft knock on another's door; we invite in and desire to enter. Peacemaking requires action; therefore, we must act in ways that open our arms and reach out to those with whom we need to reconcile.

Even as peacemaking requires action, it also requires waiting. I must wait for a response, anticipating that you will open your arms. Waiting is the part of embrace we do for another's sake, for his or her integrity. We wait because the other may not wish to be embraced at all, and embrace never forcefully breaks the boundaries of another. Embrace occurs because the desire is mutual. Waiting acknowledges that reciprocity is required to reach the goal of embrace. Peacemakers are in it for the long haul. Our open arms may not immediately be met with corresponding open arms; but embrace cannot be forced, so we are patient as we wait for God to work in the heart of the other.

When our waiting is met with reciprocity, when the arms of another open to receive us, we move to the third element of embrace, closing our arms. This is the goal of embrace, and reciprocity is the key to our understanding:

It takes *two* pairs of arms for *one* embrace; with one pair, we will either have merely an invitation to embrace (if the self respects the other) or a taking in one's clutches (if there is no such respect). In an embrace a host is a guest and a guest is a host. Though one self may receive or give more than the other, each must enter the space of the other, feel the presence of the other in the self, and make its own presence felt. Without such reciprocity, there is no embrace. (Volf, *Exclusion and Embrace*, 143)

Reciprocity is not the only requirement for this third element of embrace; gentleness is also imperative. We are not interested in "bear hugs," where the grip is too tight and there is the possibility of either side being crushed by the other.

Finally, we open our arms once more. Embrace doesn't create one body out of two. I don't lose myself to you, nor do you lose yourself to me. Embrace is successful when both sides, having been intimately connected by arms placed around each other, ultimately let go, retaining the fullness of their own identities. While we have been enriched by each other, we have not given up our uniquely created, God-given character. Letting go, however, doesn't signal the end, because the same arms that let go are the arms that opened to allow embrace. The end of one embrace signals the possibility of another, so that the movement of embrace is circular, to the other and back, to the other and back, without end.

As we engage in the hard work of reconciliation and claim Jesus' promise to peacemakers, we must recognize that we all are connected to one another. For Christ's followers, that means the metaphor of embrace includes not just friends but also enemies. Indeed, the call to be peacemakers relates specifically to our relationships with those who would be against us. Volf describes what that commitment looks like:

For the self shaped by the cross of Christ and the life of the triune God, however, embrace includes not just the other who is a friend but also the other who is the enemy. Such a self will seek to open its arms toward the other even when the other holds a sword. The other will, of course, have to drop the sword, maybe even have the sword taken out of his hand, before the actual embrace can take place. Yet even the struggle over the sword will be undergirded by the will to embrace the other and be embraced in return. (Volf, *Exclusion and Embrace*, 146)

There is no greater honor than to be considered a child of God. That distinction is promised as a blessing to those who strive to be peacemakers. Peacemaking is an undertaking of great magnitude and complexity, but with great reward: the blessedness of being called children of God because we have acted like God.

Reflecting and Recording

If you are a part of a group that meets today, note questions and issues you wish to discuss.

The four steps toward peace—or embrace—are listed here. In the space underneath each, note some actions you might take to bring reconciliation in a particular situation.

1. Opening our arms

2. Waiting

3. Closing our arms

4. Opening our arms again

If you don't have a personal relationship to which this exercise applies, think of a situation involving others. Consider what actions you might take to become an "instrument of peace," one who facilitates reconciliation, in this situation.

During the Day

Begin to put the "embrace" into practice. Pray the prayer from page 88.

✠
Group Meeting
for Week Seven

Leader: You will need a dry-erase board or newsprint for this session.

Introduction

Last week you may have discussed whether your group wants to continue meeting. If so, here are some possibilities to consider:

1.   Select two or three weeks of the workbook that were especially difficult or meaningful. Repeat those weeks in more depth to extend your time together.
2.   Decide to continue meeting as a group, using another resource. Appoint two or three members to bring resource suggestions to the group next week.
3.   One or two persons may decide to recruit and lead another group through this workbook. Many people are looking for a small-group experience, and this is a way to respond to their need.

Sharing Together

1.   Lead the group to pray aloud the prayer attributed to Saint Francis (pp. 53–54).
2.   You have only one more group meeting for this workbook. Invite two or three persons to share what this experience has meant to them thus far.
3.   On Day 1 of this week you were asked to think of the need for peacemakers in certain spheres of life: family, community, nation, world. List each category on a dry-erase board or newsprint; go through each category, inviting persons to name and describe in a word or phrase tensions and conflicts in that area. Make no comments but keep the list for the discussion that will come throughout this session.
4.   Spend eight to ten minutes discussing how inner-personal conflict can result in interpersonal conflict. Can someone in the group give a concrete example of this from his or her own life? Other than "road rage," what expressions of the connection between inner-personal and interpersonal conflict do you see? Has the news recently covered such happenings?
5.   Invite the group to name persons in the community, nation, and world who are peacemakers. Can the group agree on two, three, or four names?

6. Invite someone to read the paragraph from Day 3 that begins, "If we are to be peacemakers. . . ." Then spend six to eight minutes discussing the claim "we must guard ourselves against a spirit of vengeance in response to the evil we experience."

7. Invite volunteers to share an experience where they sought to "avenge" or "repay" some wrong done to them and it did no good.

8. Invite one or two persons to share an experience when they sought to forgive, to respond to evil with good, not to "repay" but to seek reconciliation—and the result of that effort.

9. To follow Jesus is never to react passively in the face of injustice, abuse, or undeserved suffering. As you look at the conflicts you listed in the family and in your community, can you think of persons who are acting positively to bring peace in these conflicts? (You may want to refer to your Reflecting and Recording on Day 5.) Spend a few minutes discussing what is necessary for peace to prevail and what role individuals and congregations may play in peacemaking.

10. Paul urged us to "have the mind of Christ." Keeping in mind that "in one act—the Cross—Jesus stands in solidarity with all victims and at the same time offers forgiveness and atonement to all perpetrators," spend ten to twelve minutes discussing the following questions:
    a. In what ways do the three peacemakers you named earlier confirm this statement?
    b. In what way can the dynamic of the Cross be brought to bear upon the national and world conflicts you listed earlier?
    c. Are we willing to trust redemptive suffering as the core dynamic of peacemaking?

11. Spend a few minutes reviewing Days 6 and 7. Then spend the rest of your time discussing the following:
    a. the necessity of abandoning the categories of oppressed and oppressor—especially in the conflicts of our community and nation.
    b. the essentials for you as individuals and your congregation to accept the "embrace" that makes for peace.

Praying Together

Structure your prayer time in the following way: Invite one person to pray for peace in the family, asking for any special requests before the prayer. Then ask another person to focus on community, another on the nation, and another on the world.

Close as you began—by praying together the prayer attributed to Saint Francis.

Week Eight

The Crown of Righteousness

DAY 1

Persecution Is Alive and Well in Our World

Blessed are those who are persecuted for righteousness' sake, for theirs is the kingdom of heaven.

Blessed are you when people revile you and persecute you and utter all kinds of evil against you falsely on my account. Rejoice and be glad, for your reward is great in heaven, for in the same way they persecuted the prophets who were before you. (Matt. 5:10-11)

In April 2003 we attended a World Evangelism gathering at which Maimunah Natasha, a Methodist businesswoman from Indonesia, spoke. Mai is a dear friend who is committed to the cause of Christ in her homeland. She related story after story of persecution experienced by Christians in Indonesia. Time and again she pleaded for our prayers and support.

Believing in the gospel of Jesus Christ can be a life-threatening experience in Indonesia. The government requires everyone to carry an identification card that includes information about religious status. Roadblocks have been set up to check identification cards, and men have been dragged from their vehicles and chopped into pieces when authorities discover that they profess faith in Christ. In the last decade, over five hundred churches in Indonesia have been burned. Prison, torture, and death are common occurrences.

As we listened to Mai's experience, we felt grateful for the religious freedom we experience in the United States. Yet alongside that gratitude was also a sense of distance. Because we don't have to worry about experiencing violence because of our faith, it's difficult to understand that experience. Because we seldom hear stories of persecution, it is easy to begin to think of persecution as something that happens only in some distant place to a distant people or, worse still, something that occurred only in Bible times. Because we are separated from the experience of religious persecution, able to worship without fear, it is easy to become complacent and take our faith for granted. Yet Jesus tells us that it is not those who worship with ease and in safety who will inherit the kingdom of heaven; it is not those who have never suffered on behalf of their faith. It is the persecuted, those who have experienced pain and fear, prison, and even death because of their love for the Lord whom God will bless and honor with God's kingdom.

What, then, are we to make of Jesus' words of blessing for the persecuted? What message is there for those of us who have spent our lives worshiping in freedom—unaccosted and secure? One answer can be found in Hebrews 13:3: "Remember those who are in prison, as though you were in prison with them; those who are being tortured, as though you yourselves were being tortured." We must stand in solidarity with our brothers and sisters who suffer for their faith. We must remember them and be willing to enter into their pain.

To be sure, the blood of the martyrs is the seed of the church. But not only so: the suffering of the faithful is the constant and abiding inspiration for the church's courage and witness.

While many of us practice our faith in safety, Christians all over the world, in rare instances even in the United States, have been and continue to suffer because of their commitment to Jesus Christ. In April 2002, the United Nations Commission on Human Rights released the following report:

> We estimate that there are more than 200 million Christians in the world today who do not have full human rights as defined by the Universal Declaration of Human Rights, simply because they are Christians. . . . We believe that this is the largest group in the world without full human rights because of their beliefs. (Johan Candelin, Director of the WEA Religious Liberty Commission, quotation provided by Voice of the Martyrs, www. persecution.com)

Reflecting and Recording

Name here two persons you know who have suffered most for their faith.

Make some notes about them and the nature of their suffering. Were they persecuted? Did their suffering result from their belief and/or action? Did their living the Christian life threaten the way of life of those around them?

Have you ever experienced danger as a result of your commitment to Christ? Reflect on that experience.

■ ■ ■

Pray about that experience, thanking God for delivering you from the danger. If you have not experienced such danger, thank God for that mercy and focus on those in the world who regularly face danger because of their faith.

■ ■ ■

If you wish to explore the topic of religious persecution more thoroughly, here are two books that will help.

- *By Their Blood: Christian Martyrs of the Twentieth Century*, James C. and Marti Hefley (Baker Books, 2001)
- *Jesus Freaks: Stories of Those Who Stood for Jesus*, dc Talk and The Voice of the Martyrs (Bethany House, 1999)

During the Day

Before each meal today, remember and pray for the persons you named above. If you know persons in prison, remember them "as though you were in prison with them; those who are being tortured [persecuted in any way] as though you yourselves were being tortured."

DAY 2

There, Not Here; Them, Not Us

Just as the body is one and has many members, and all the members of the body, though many, are one body, so it is with Christ. For in the one Spirit we were all baptized into one body—Jews or Greeks, slaves or free—and we were all made to drink of one Spirit.

Indeed, the body does not consist of one member but of many. . . . If one member suffers, all suffer together with it; if one member is honored, all rejoice together with it.

Now you are the body of Christ and individually members of it. (1 Cor. 12:12-14, 26-27)

The persecution and penalties suffered by early Christians were terrible. History tells us that some Christians were fed to lions and burned at the stake. Compared to other atrocities, these methods of persecution may have been a welcomed alternative. Nero bound Christians to stakes, wrapped them in pitch, and set them afire to be living torches to light his gardens. Demonic imagination created suffering as awfully torturous as possible: molten lead poured upon them; red-hot plates attached to the tenderest parts of their bodies; parts of their body cut off and roasted before their eyes; eyes torn out; hands and feet burned while cold water was poured on them to extend the agony.

It is hard for modern Christians to imagine what those first Christians had to suffer. It may be even more difficult to accept the fact that suffering and persecution just as grotesque remain alive in our world today. As was true in the past, persecution gives testimony to the church's faithfulness.

The number of deaths currently resulting from belief in Jesus Christ is unparalleled. We frequently think of martyrdom as a phenomenon from those early days of the church; yet according to *World Mission Digest*, in the twentieth century close to *one hundred million* people were martyred for their faith in Jesus Christ. This figure may be greater than the number of people martyred in all the previous nineteen centuries combined. (Hefley, *By Their Blood*, 589)

The reality of religious persecution is that it is not something that happens there, not here; it is not something that happens to them, not us. As Christians we are the body of Christ. This was Paul's vivid understanding of the church: "Just as the body is one and has many members, and all the members of the body, though many, are one body, so it is with Christ" (1 Cor. 12:12). In an almost humorous way, Paul makes the case for our oneness as "the body" by posing imaginary conversation among the members of the physical body: "If the foot would say, 'Because I am not a hand, I do not belong to the body,' that would not make it any less a part of the body" (1 Cor. 12:15). Then his humor really becomes pronounced: "If the whole body were an eye, where would the hearing be? If the whole body were hearing, where would the sense of smell be?" (1 Cor. 12:17)

Each Christian is a member of the body of Christ. That means "If one member suffers, all suffer together with it; if one member is honored, all rejoice together with it" (v. 26).

In The United Methodist Church, during the Great Thanksgiving portion of the Communion liturgy, we pray:

Pour out your Holy Spirit on us gathered here,
    and on these gifts of bread and wine.
Make them be for us the body and blood of Christ,
that we may be *for the world* the body of Christ,
    redeemed by his blood.
By your Spirit make us *one with Christ,*
    one with each other,

and *one in ministry to all the world,*
until Christ comes in final victory
    and we feast at his heavenly banquet.
("A Service of Word and Table I," *The United Methodist Hymnal,* 10, emphasis ours)

As one body, we must heed the word of Hebrews 13:3 and remember those suffering for their faith as though we too were suffering, those in prison as though we were in prison with them, and those being tortured and even killed as though we ourselves were being tortured and faced death because of our commitment to Christ.

Reflecting and Recording

What has been your greatest challenge to practicing your faith? Make some brief notes.

For most of us, the challenge to our faith has not been overt persecution or physical suffering. We will consider this topic more tomorrow. For now spend a few minutes reflecting on how the following words of scripture instruct and guide you.

> Even if you do suffer for doing what is right, you are blessed. Do not fear what they fear, and do not be intimidated, but in your hearts sanctify Christ as Lord. Always be ready to make your defense to anyone who demands from you an accounting for the hope that is in you; yet do it with gentleness and reverence. Keep your conscience clear, so that, when you are maligned, those who abuse you for your good conduct in Christ may be put to shame. For it is better to suffer for doing good, if suffering should be God's will, than to suffer for doing evil. (1 Pet. 3:14-17)

■ ■ ■

Spend the balance of your time pondering the implication of these petitions from the Great Thanksgiving:

"[May we be] for the world the body of Christ, redeemed by his blood."

■ ■ ■

"Make us one with Christ, one with each other, and one in ministry to all the world."

■ ■ ■

During the Day

A portion of the Great Thanksgiving is adapted and printed on page 209 (it is labeled Prayer for Persecuted Christians). Cut it out, carry it with you for four or five days, and pray it at your noonday meal and other times that come to mind.

If you have Internet access, visit the website for The Voice of the Martyrs at www.persecution.com. When you arrive at the site, click on the link labeled *prisoner list*, which will provide you with information about writing to persons who have been imprisoned for their faith or to the governments responsible. Act on one of the suggestions provided.

DAY 3

Persecution: A Holy Word

The time is coming when people will not put up with sound doctrine, but having itching ears, they will accumulate for themselves teachers to suit their own desires, and will turn away from listening to the truth and wander away to myths. (2 Tim. 4:3-4)

One of Jesus' character traits was sheer honesty. He did not seek to hide the costs of following him or soft-pedal the demands of discipleship. He left no doubt about what might happen to those who responded to his call. In this Beatitude, Jesus names three "sufferings" that are the lot of faithful disciples: reproach (an expression of rebuke or disapproval), persecution, and slander. Luke's rendering expresses this Beatitude a bit differently: "Blessed are you when people hate you, and when they exclude you, revile you, and defame you on account of the Son of Man" (Luke 6:22).

Jesus, the servant Messiah, knows that those who serve him will suffer as he suffered. While most Christians in the United States and the West have not known much suffering for their faith, this may not always be the case. Already in the United States, the separation of church and state is used as an argument to prohibit almost every public profession of the Christian faith. French government leaders, triggered by Muslim female students wearing the head scarf (*hijab*), recently prohibited any sign of religious identification on persons. They also banned the public wearing of yarmulkes by Jews and "large" crosses by Christians. A new kind of persecution is emerging. Hatred, defaming, exclusion, reviling—the words Jesus used—are becoming attitudinal responses to and actions against Christians.

But let's keep perspective. Yesterday we explored the fact that the persecution of Christians is a real phenomenon, not just something that occurred in the distant past. Because we are one in the body of Christ, we are called upon to share in the suffering of others through solidarity with them. We need to understand clearly the definition of persecution so that we avoid an exaggerated perception of our own difficulties. While our society may be hostile, while we may be living in a "culture of disbelief," as author Stephen Carter refers to it, our hardships hardly rise to the level of the martyrs' through the ages.

Persecution is a powerful and holy word that probably should be reserved for those who truly experience pain and suffering. Being denied the opportunity to share our faith at a high school graduation ceremony, or prohibited from mailing Bible studies or religious comic books to soldiers stationed in Iraq, or even losing a job for sharing the gospel—all these are unjust circumstances that warrant strong response from the Christian community. However, we cannot with integrity compare them to the persecution experienced by the Indonesian Christians mentioned in Day 1, who have seen loved ones pulled from cars and shot or hacked to death because of their commitment to Christ. Whenever we exaggerate our own difficulties, contriving persecution where there is only challenge, we trivialize the genuine persecution occurring to Christians in other parts of the world. We may live in a culture of disbelief where anti-Christian bias abounds; we may experience injustice or discrimination or even feel that liberalism has simply run amok; but the reality is that presently in the United States there are no formal liabilities connected with being Christian—each of us has access to courts of law and public opinion where our grievances can be heard. As long as that remains the case, we are wise to face our spiritual challenges with strength and integrity and reserve the holy word *persecution* for those who suffer and die for their faith.

While claiming loyalty to Christ leads to persecution for some people but not others, for all who profess their faith and actively pursue the Christian life, disruption occurs. For the early Christians, disruption was inevitable. Most jobs and business interests conflicted with their faithfulness to Jesus.

The early Christians' newfound faith certainly disrupted their social life. In that ancient world, most of the feasts were held in the temple of some god. Not all the animals being sacrificed were burned on the altar. William Barclay reminds us:

> Part of the meat went to the priests as their perquisite; and part of the meat was returned to the worshipper. With his share he made a feast for his friends and his relations. One of the gods most commonly worshipped was Serapis. And when the invitations to the feast went out, they would read: "I invite you to dine with me at the table of our Lord Serapis."
>
> Could a Christian share in a feast held in the temple of a heathen god? Even an ordinary meal in an ordinary house began with a libation, a cup of wine, poured out in honour of the gods. It was like grace before meat. Could a Christian become a sharer in a heathen act of worship like that? (Barclay, *The Gospel of Matthew*, rev. ed., 1:111–12)

Perhaps the worst disruption for early Christians took place in their home life. One member of a family became a Christian when others did not: a wife but not the husband, a son or daughter but not the parents. Immediately the family was splintered. The "new" Christian was banished. "It was literally true that a man might have to love Christ more than he loved father or mother, wife, or brother or sister." (Barclay, *The Gospel of Matthew*, rev. ed., 1:112) Like early Christians, we can experience disruption when we commit ourselves to Christ; and, regardless of our circumstances, we are called to be faithful just as they were.

Reflecting and Recording

Some readers may have experienced genuine persecution because of their Christianity. But not most of us. In our work, maybe; in our social life, perhaps; in our home life, possibly. Look at your own experience. If you have known disruption, suffering, oppression, exclusion, slander, reproach, or hatred on account of your commitment and loyalty to Christ, make notes about these in the three categories listed:

Work/business life

Social life

Home life

If you have not experienced persecution in one of the areas above, name someone who has (in the appropriate space), and make some notes about that person's experience.

■ ■ ■

Spend some time pondering the following question: If I were more faithful to Christ in my work/business/social life, would I experience persecution?

■ ■ ■

In what relationships—business, social, family—am I reserved in my Christian witness because I fear exclusion, reproach, slander, or even hatred or persecution?

■ ■ ■

During the Day

If you did not check the website or write or call The Voice of the Martyrs yesterday, do so today.

Check yourself today—in your work, family, and social contacts—to see if you are holding back in your Christian witness and faithfulness because of fear.

Continue to use the Prayer for Persecuted Christians.

DAY 4

House of Cards

When some were speaking about the temple, how it was adorned with beautiful stones and gifts dedicated to God, [Jesus] said, "As for these things that you see, the days will come when not one stone will be left upon another; all will be thrown down. (Luke 21:5-6)

Have you ever built a house of cards? It can be delicate work: one slight bump and the entire structure comes crashing down. When that happens, we're usually not too surprised. We don't put much faith in houses of cards. Unfortunately, we put great faith in other structures: our government, our jobs, the security of our nation, our homes, our material possessions, our families, and even our churches. Usually we don't realize how much faith we have placed in these human structures until they come crashing down around us.

On September 10, 2001, few people in the United States worried about national security. Like every other day of their lives, people went to work and school, traveled on airplanes, enjoyed spending time with family and friends. Yet within a mere twenty-four hours, that sense of security, that faith in the intrinsic safety of our nation, was destroyed. The events of September 11 illustrated in tragically vivid terms the transient nature of everything human. Even as Americans have sought to fight terrorism since 9/11, we have seen time and again the fallacy of placing our faith in human structures. Afghanistan remains a breeding ground for terrorists even without the Taliban's official leadership. The war in Iraq brought neither peace nor stability to the Middle East, and more U.S. military personnel have been killed or wounded since the war was declared over than in the official conflict itself.

Governments are not the only human structures in which we place our faith. Our material possessions claim much of our allegiance. Our networks of family and friends, our jobs, our churches—all of these lay hold of our hearts. Yet these are human structures, many blessed by God, but human nonetheless. And because we place so much faith in them, when they fall, we are easily crushed. Friendships become estranged; marriages crumble; jobs are eliminated; debt smothers; churches reveal themselves not as the safe and supportive places we believed them to be but as communities filled with flawed and less-than-perfect individuals just like us.

The tendency to place our faith and hope in things that are unworthy is what Jesus was talking about in Luke 21:5-6. In saying, "As for these things that you see, the days will come when not one stone will be left upon another; all will be thrown down," Jesus warned us against becoming terrified or overwhelmed when worldly structures crumble. Regardless of the structures—economic or political, religious or even family—like a house of cards, they are not worthy of our confidence. We do not need to place our faith and hope in the various "houses of cards" we construct in this world but in the only sure foundation: the kingdom of God, realized both now and in the future. When we place our faith in worthy things—God and God's kingdom—Jesus promises a reward: we will share in God's victory.

In speaking of God's blessing the persecuted, Jesus highlights the facts that life is difficult and that being faithful is costly. Persecution is terrible, but unfaithfulness is much worse. The world would have us place our faith in it and often counters our efforts to place our faith in God; yet Jesus tells us that God is on our side when we suffer. Those who persevere through hardship, keeping their faith in God, will inherit God's kingdom. They "will see the Son of Man arrive on the clouds of heaven with power and great glory. And he will send forth his angels with the sound of a mighty trumpet blast, and they will gather together his chosen ones from the farthest ends of the earth and heaven" (Matt. 24:30-31, NLT).

Reflecting and Recording

Has any human structure in which you placed your faith become a "house of cards" and crashed? Describe that experience.

Recall and describe an experience in which you persevered through hardship. What blessings resulted? How did you experience the presence and strength of Christ?

List three persons you know who are suffering or going through particular hardships.

Close your time by praying specifically for these persons.

During the Day

Insert the names of these three persons in the Prayer for Persecuted Christians. When you pray the prayer, remember these persons.

DAY 5

Don't Give Up

Then they will hand you over to be tortured and will put you to death, and you will be hated by all nations because of my name. Then many will fall away, and they will betray one another and hate one another. And many false prophets will arise and lead many astray. And because of the increase of lawlessness, the love of many will grow cold. But the one who endures to the end will be saved. And this good news of the kingdom will be proclaimed throughout the world, as a testimony to all the nations; and then the end will come. (Matt. 24:9-14)

Yesterday we talked about placing our faith and hope in things worthy of faith and hope. Jesus warns that if we choose to follow him, life will be difficult. Often, as in the passage above, those warnings are harsh.

The early church obviously took Jesus' warnings to heart. They had experienced many of the situations Jesus mentions. In 70 CE, the Temple in Jerusalem was destroyed, never to be rebuilt. This was a cataclysmic event, as the Temple was the center of Jewish faith. It had been destroyed in 587 BCE when the Jews were exiled to Babylon. Through faith and perseverance the Jews began to rebuild the Temple on a smaller scale when they returned from exile in 538 BCE. In 37 BCE Herod the Great was appointed as ruler over Palestine, and work began on expanding the Temple to make it a magnificent center of worship and Jewish life. The expansion was finally completed in 64 CE, a mere six years before the Temple's complete destruction. False prophets were prevalent, as were wars and natural disasters. Christians were persecuted by the Roman government and the Jewish hierarchy.

It was a dangerous time to proclaim faith in Jesus Christ, yet the church responded by trusting Christ and bracing themselves for inevitable trouble, never giving up. That serves as a key lesson for us. *The church was not surprised by tribulation.* Nowhere do the letters of Paul, for example, indicate that he or the churches to which he wrote were shocked or disillusioned by the difficulties they encountered. Trials and difficulties were an expected part of the coming of the kingdom of God. Rather than becoming disillusioned, early Christians responded to trouble by enduring in faith and establishing a new spiritual community.

What about today? If there is no tension between the church and the world, we have reason either for celebration or concern. One of two situations has occurred: (1) The world has been completely converted to Christ, and we can celebrate, or (2) The church has watered down and compromised her message, and we'd better be concerned. It's easy for us to succumb to doubt and disappointment when faced with tribulation and suffering. It's easy to become cynical about faith and God's connection to our lives. Condoleezza Rice, National Security Advisor for the Bush administration (2001–2004), spoke against that temptation in a sermon at Menlo Park Presbyterian Church:

> Struggle and sorrow are not license to give way to self-doubt, to self-pity, and to defeat, [but are] an opportunity to find a renewed spirit and a renewed strength to carry on. [How else but through struggle] are we to get to know the full measure of the Lord's capacity for intervention in our lives? If there are no burdens, how can we know that he can be there to lift them? (Condoleezza Rice, "The Privilege of Struggle" as quoted in Sheryl Henderson Blunt, "The Unflappable Condi Rice: Why the World's Most Powerful Woman Asks God for Help," *Christianity Today*, [September 2003]: 42–48)

Jesus' words about persecution and suffering reflect hope, not cynicism. He promises that we will inherit God's kingdom when we remain faithful through pain and tragedy, suffering and trial. Jesus' promise that God blesses those who are persecuted underscores what Rice refers to as the privilege of struggle. Those who endure; those whose faith remains steadfast; those who, even in the most horrendous conditions, continue to raise their voices to God in loyalty and faith—those persons will be gathered from the ends of the earth when the Son of Man comes in his glory. The earliest followers of Christ built the church on that faith. We must rest our faith on that same foundation.

Reflecting and Recording

What struggle or tribulation tempts you to succumb to self-doubt, self-pity, or cynicism? Make a few notes here:

How might Jesus' promise that God blesses those who are persecuted help you overcome temptation to self-doubt, self-pity, or cynicism?

Reread the quotation from Condoleezza Rice's sermon. Spend the rest of your time pondering her two questions.

During the Day

Remain aware of the temptation to give in to feelings of self-doubt or self-pity. When they come, name them and pray for the Lord to banish them from you. Continue to use the Prayer for Persecuted Christians, inserting the names of people you know or names from The Voice of the Martyrs website.

DAY 6

Mighty Powers of Darkness

Be strong in the Lord and in the strength of his power. Put on the whole armor of God, so that you may be able to stand against the wiles of the devil. For our struggle is not against enemies of blood and flesh, but against the rulers, against the authorities, against the cosmic powers of this present darkness, against the spiritual forces of evil in the heavenly places. (Eph. 6:10-12)

One of the twentieth century's shortcomings was its failure to realize the significance of the spirit. Education, science, and technological advancement became elevated to the exclusion of the spiritual realm; these areas were focused on as the means for the world to become a better, saner place. Yet Nazi Germany, one of the most educated nations of the twentieth century—whose scientists provided rocket technology for Russia and the United States—was the same country that created a highly organized system to exterminate eleven million people. Clearly, education, science, and technology, divorced from the reality of the spirit, are not the panaceas we once thought them to be.

Underlying Jesus' promise that God blesses those who are persecuted is the knowledge that persecution and evil are powerful forces in the world, and they are connected. Jesus understood the power of evil; he knew that this force would not disappear entirely until God's kingdom was fully realized. He knew that until that time there would always be persecution and suffering and tribulation and fear. We moderns have not succeeded in eradicating these situations from our world; the answer does not involve having more money, more knowledge, or more technology. Rather, it concerns recognizing the spiritual nature of evil. As we suffer, as we seek to stand in solidarity with those who are persecuted (as Jesus did), as we fight against the evil that seeks to inflict pain and persecution, we must recognize that we are fighting against a spirit of hate whose entire purpose is to destroy people. This spirit defies logic. Jesus urged us to recognize this fact when he said, "Dear friends, don't be afraid of those who want to kill you. They can only kill the body; they cannot do any more to you" (Luke 12:4, NLT). Jesus understood that the real enemy is not people, although people bear responsibility for untold destruction and suffering. The real enemy is much more powerful than people. We can kill those who persecute us, but the real enemy will always rise again, using others for its purposes. The real enemy is the mighty power of darkness, the spirit of evil that defies logic. This spirit of evil can be tragically obvious as it expresses itself in the ways Jesus named active persecution: "when people hate you . . . exclude you . . . revile you . . . defame you" (Luke 6:22).

In October 1998, twenty-one-year-old Matthew Shepard of Casper, Wyoming, was tied to a fence, beaten unconscious, and left to die on the outskirts of Laramie. He died five days later. The motivation for this hate crime was Shepard's sexual orientation—he was gay. Outside his funeral Reverend Fred Phelps, from Topeka, Kansas, carried signs proclaiming, "God Hates Fags."

In October 2003, Reverend Phelps attempted to place a six-foot granite monument in a park in Casper. The proposed monument would include a bronze plaque with Shepard's image and the words, "Matthew Shepard entered hell October 12, 1998, at age 21 in defiance of God's solemn warning." The Casper city council rejected Phelps's request. ("Town rejects 'Shepard in hell' monument," Web log dated October 29, 2003, Eric Johnston, Gay.com/PlanetOut.com Network)

Often evil is not so tragically obvious. More often it is dangerously subtle. Succumbing to its influence is easy, especially when we are spiritually complacent.

The spirit of hate is an equal opportunity employer—it cares nothing for your race, creed, gender, age, or physical ability. That is why, while we can kill or lash out at those who attack us, persecute us, or cause us pain, we will never be able to obliterate the mighty spirit of darkness—because every day more people are subtly persuaded by its influence. That is also why battling evil is not simply a matter of education or economic development. We are fighting a powerful spirit, and the danger is not simply physical but also spiritual. People infected with the spirit of evil may produce physical pain and even death, but as Jesus said, they can only kill the body. The greater danger is spiritual death, a process that begins when evil infects our spirits with hate, fear, and prejudice.

Reflecting and Recording

Look back over the past year. What is the most blatant expression of evil you remember? Make a few notes, jotting down as many details as possible.

Now focus on your personal life during the past year. Was there an event, experience, season of struggle, or relationship in which evil was clearly at work? Make some notes to get in touch with that experience.

Go back and read Ephesians 6:10-12, the passage we began with today. Spend the rest of your time reflecting on it and how that text is confirmed in the public and personal expressions you have recorded.

During the Day

If you know someone undergoing a debilitating, threatening struggle, contact and encourage him or her. If appropriate, remind this person that the "powers of darkness" are at work, and we can resist them through the power of Christ.

Today or in the next few days, engage someone in a discussion about our fight with evil. Share with them your use of this workbook and the emphasis on persecution.

✠

DAY 7

Me and Mine

We live as human beings, but we do not wage war according to human standards; for the weapons of our warfare are not merely human, but they have divine power to destroy strongholds. We destroy arguments and every proud obstacle raised up against the knowledge of God, and we take every thought captive to obey Christ. We are ready to punish every disobedience when your obedience is complete. (2 Cor. 10:3-6)

The movie O *Brother, Where Art Thou?* tells about the strange experiences of three escaped convicts running from the law. In one memorable scene, Everett, Delmar, and Pete are trapped in a barn by the sheriff's posse that has been chasing them. They peer out of the barn and see Wash, Pete's cousin, who has led the posse to them in exchange for bounty money. Standing outside the barn, Wash shouts, "Sorry, Pete! I know we're kin, but they got this depression on. I got to do for me and mine."

The inclination to divide the world into "me and mine" is natural. Yet it is also the tool for evil. Cleverly capitalizing on our natural instinct to "do for me and mine," evil triggers an insidious domino effect. Arab Americans continue to suffer a painful backlash in the wake of 9/11. Japanese Americans were forced into internment camps during World War II. Racial profiling is used on highways and in airports. The truth that becomes hidden from us is that the real enemy is not a person or group of people but a spirit of hate that blames others and uses fear to manipulate us into seeing them as enemies.

James M. Wall highlighted the insidious nature of evil during the keynote address at the 2002 Boston Wesleyan Association Religion Symposium. He said:

Doing for me and mine is a natural instinct; but how we define "me and mine" is a measure of our soul's relationship with God. . . .

We are engaged in a titanic struggle of Us against Them, and no matter what our leaders tell us, Them is winning, because they have forced us to define ourselves as a people whose soul is focused from our dark side. (Wall, "The Future of a Vision: Religious Journalism in a Post–9/11 World," the 2002 Boston Wesleyan Association Religion Symposium Keynote Address, September 28, 2002, Cambridge, Massachusetts, reprinted in *Zion's Herald*, 176:5–6)

Jesus proclaimed that God blesses those who are persecuted. If evil works in our hearts and minds, subtly moving us to distinguish between Us and Them, then we risk becoming perpetrators of persecution and injustice. Jesus' word, then, is not just a message of promise and hope for those who are suffering; it is also a warning for those, including us, who may be defining themselves from their "dark side," succumbing to a spirit of hate that uses fear and manipulation to destroy others.

A bumper sticker caught our attention: "We are creating enemies faster then we can kill them." If Wall is correct and how we define *me* and *mine* serves as a measure of our relationship with God, then we would do well to evaluate our definitions and guard against the real enemy—not "Them" but the evil that operates out of the dark side of each of us.

This week we have focused on persecution and its foundation of evil. This can be a difficult concept to fully understand because often we do not vividly experience persecution and evil. Yet Jesus predicted that the world would hate us because it hated him first. He warned us that the world loves us when we belong to it, but if we belong to Jesus, the world will be against us (John 15:18-19). In the Beatitudes, Jesus promises to bless us through that experience.

But take note of this: Jesus' promise of blessing to the persecuted has meaning only if we determine to live in such a way that we risk experiencing persecution—acting as radical agents of love in contrast to a world founded on force. Unfortunately we often avoid those risks because the ease of practicing our faith (or not practicing it) blinds us to the reality that we are at war with evil—evil resulting from our own choices to go against the created order of God, evil created every time we ignore God because we think we have a better way, evil that ultimately results in destruction in someone's life.

We must claim God's promise of victory—not through force, but through the Cross. Jesus undertook the amazing risk of the Cross, submitted himself to the terror of evil, and provided a victory that stands in complete contrast to the world. Evil works through force, but God does not. God's weapons can be found in Ephesians 6:

> Stand therefore, and fasten the belt of truth around your waist, and put on the breastplate of righteousness. As shoes for your feet put on whatever will make you ready to proclaim the gospel of peace. With all of these, take the shield of faith, with which you will be able to quench all the flaming arrows of the evil one. Take the helmet of salvation, and the sword of the Spirit, which is the word of God. (vv. 14-17)

The Cross is not easy, but it is the only way. The ultimate victory has been won. The battles we have to fight in the meantime must be with the weapons of faith, hope, and love.

Reflecting and Recording

Spend a few minutes reflecting on the following "weapons" for our use in the battle against evil and persecution. How might you claim these?

shoes of the gospel of peace

■ ■ ■

shield of faith

■ ■ ■

helmet of salvation

■ ■ ■

sword of the Spirit—the word of God

■ ■ ■

If you are a part of a group, today will be your last meeting. Make some notes about issues or questions you would like to discuss.

Spend as long as you can reflecting on your eight-week journey. Write words or sentences that communicate what you have experienced, questions raised, decisions made, directions discerned, truth that has come alive. This is only for you, so make notes that will speak to you, perhaps a few months from now when you review what you have written.

During the Day

Second Corinthians 10:5 is printed on page 209. Cut it out and carry it with you in the coming days. Read it often until you memorize it, seeking to make it a guide for your life.

Group Meeting for Week Eight

Introduction

Today is the last meeting for this group study. You have talked about the possibility of continuing to meet. Conclude those plans. Whatever you choose to do, determine the actual time line so that participants can make a clear commitment. Assign some persons to follow through with decisions made.

Sharing Together

During this session, reflect on the entire eight-week experience. ***Leader:*** Save enough time for responses to questions 12 and 13, as well as adequate time for prayer.

1. Invite someone to read 1 Corinthians 12:12-14 and 26-27, printed at the beginning of Day 2 (p. 187). Then sing a verse of a hymn you know by heart, such as "What a Friend We Have in Jesus."

2. On Day 1 you were asked to name two persons you know who have suffered most for their faith. Invite three or four people to identify one of the persons they named and describe the circumstance of their suffering.

3. Have persons in the group experienced danger as a result of their commitment to Christ? Ask for volunteers to share that experience.

4. How many persons in the group could not name someone they know who has suffered for the faith? How many have not experienced any danger as a result of their commitment to Christ? In light of these responses, do you think it is possible for us to understand the eighth Beatitude? Does our experience reveal whether we really are living the Christian faith?

5. Invite anyone who may have checked The Voice of the Martyrs website to report on his or her findings.

6. If anyone had opportunity to look at either book suggested on page 187, let that person give a brief response.

7. Spend ten to twelve minutes discussing the anti-Christian bias creeping steadily through our culture, the persecution it already brings, and the possibility that persecution will become more commonplace.

8. Spend four to five minutes discussing the claim that *persecution* is a holy word.

9. Spend eight to ten minutes sharing how we as individuals and congregations "remember those who are in prison, as though you were in prison with them; those who are being tortured, as though you yourselves were being tortured" (Heb. 13:3). Share examples of how persecution/torture may already be taking place.

10. The lives of early Christians were totally disrupted because of their faith practice. Are there areas of injustice, blatant secularizing of culture, oppressive treatment of a people or a group in our community to which, if we made a passionate and compassionate Christian response, our lives would be disrupted and we might even be persecuted? Spend some time dealing with this possibility, giving particular attention to how our practice of Christianity affects our work/business life, our social life, and even our home life.

11. Invite someone to read the last paragraph of Day 4 (p. 194, preceding Reflecting and Recording). Spend a few minutes reflecting on what this means for you as individuals and for your congregation.

12. Review the content of Day 6 and spend a few minutes discussing evil—not philosophically but in the practical expressions of evil infecting our spirits with hate, fear, hardness of heart, prejudice, and self-preoccupation.

13. Use your remaining time to reflect on the weeks you have spent together. What has this experience meant to individuals in the group—new insights, challenges, commitments? What areas of your life need changes? What issues do you need to work on?

Praying Together

Pray aloud together the words from the Great Thanksgiving on Day 2 (pp. 188–89).

1. Invite each group member to share a commitment he or she has made or specific prayer requests. As each person shares, have a time of prayer—silent or spoken, preferably spoken—so that each person will be prayed for specifically.

2. Now ask two or three people to offer general prayers of thanksgiving for the eight-week experience and petitions for further growth and guidance.

3. A benediction is a blessing or greeting shared with another person or by a group in parting. A variation on the traditional "passing of the peace" can serve as a benediction. Form a circle with group members. The leader takes the hand of the person next to him or her, looks into his or her eyes, and says,

"The peace of God be with you." That person responds, "And may God's peace be yours." Then that person takes the hand of the person next to him or her and says, "The peace of God be with you," and receives the response, "And may God's peace be yours." Continue passing the peace around the circle until everyone has opportunity to participate.

4.   After the passing of the peace, speak to one another more spontaneously. Move around to different individuals in the group, saying whatever you feel is appropriate as a parting blessing to each person. Or simply embrace the person and say nothing. In your own unique way, bless each person who has shared this journey with you.

SOURCES

Albom, Mitch. *Tuesdays with Morrie: An Old Man, a Young Man, and Life's Greatest Lesson.* New York: Doubleday, 1997.

Barclay, William. *The Gospel of Matthew.* Rev. ed. 2 vols. The Daily Study Bible Series. Philadelphia, Pa.: Westminster Press, 1975.

———. *The Letters to the Galatians and Ephesians.* Rev. ed. The Daily Study Bible Series. Philadelphia, Pa.: Westminster Press, 1976.

Bauman, Zygmunt. *Life in Fragments: Essays in Postmodern Morality.* Oxford: Blackwell, 1995.

Blunt, Sheryl Henderson. "The Unflappable Condi Rice: Why the World's Most Powerful Woman Asks God for Help." *Christianity Today* (September 2003): 42–48.

Boreham, F. W. *The Heavenly Octave: A Study of the Beatitudes.* New York: Abingdon Press, 1936.

Bowden, Mark. "Tales of the Tyrant." *Atlantic Monthly* 289, no. 5 (May 2002): 35.

Bragg, Rick. *All Over but the Shoutin'.* New York: Pantheon Books, 1997.

Carretto, Carlo. *I, Francis.* Translated by Robert R. Barr. Maryknoll, N.Y.: Orbis Books, 1982.

———. *I Sought and I Found: My Experience of God and of the Church.* Translated by Robert Barr. Maryknoll, N.Y.: Orbis Books, 1984.

Carter, Stephen L. *The Culture of Disbelief: How American Law and Politics Trivialize Religious Devotion.* New York: Basic Books, 1993.

Connell, Ruth, comp. *The Secret of Happiness: Matthew 5.* Minneapolis, Minn.: Winston Press, 1985.

Dunnam, Maxie D. *Be Your Whole Self.* Old Tappan, N.J.: Fleming H. Revell Company, 1970.

Galloway, Kathy. *Struggles to Love: The Spirituality of the Beatitudes.* London: Society for Promoting Christian Knowledge, 1994.

George, Timothy, and Alister McGrath, eds. *For All the Saints: Evangelical Theology and Christian Spirituality.* Louisville, Ky.: Westminster John Knox Press, 2003.

Harnish, James A. *Journey to the Center of the Faith: An Explorer's Guide to Christian Living.* Nashville, Tenn.: Abingdon Press, 2001.

———. *You Only Have to Die: Leading Your Congregation to New Life.* Nashville, Tenn.: Abingdon Press, 2004.

Hefley, James C., and Marti Hefley. *By Their Blood: Christian Martyrs of the 20th Century.* Milford, Mich.: Mott Media, 1979.

Hunter, Archibald M. *A Pattern for Life: An Exposition of the Sermon on the Mount, Its Making, Its Exegesis and Its Meaning.* Rev. ed. Philadelphia, Pa.: Westminster Press, 1965.

Jordan, Clarence. *Sermon on the Mount*. Valley Forge, Pa.: Judson Press, Koinonia Publication, 1970.

King, Martin Luther, Jr. *A Testament of Hope: The Essential Writings and Speeches of Martin Luther King, Jr.* Edited by James Melvin Washington. San Francisco: HarperSanFrancisco, 1986.

Kinlaw, Dennis F. *The Mind of Christ*. Nappanee, Ind.: Francis Asbury Press, 1998.

Langford, Andy, and Mark Ralls. *Beginnings: An Introduction to Christian Faith*. Nashville, Tenn.: Abingdon Press, 2003.

Law, William. *The Works of the Reverend William Law*. Vol. 9, *Of Justification by Faith and Works: A Dialogue between a Methodist and a Churchman*. 2nd ed. London: J. Richardson, 1762.

Lewis, C. S. *The Four Loves*. San Diego, Calif.: Harcourt Brace & Company, 1988.

———. *The Weight of Glory and Other Addresses*. Rev. ed. Edited by Walter Hooper. New York: Macmillan Publishing Company, 1980.

Lucado, Max. *The Applause of Heaven*. Dallas, Tex.: Word Publishing, 1995.

Manning, Brennan. *Ruthless Trust: The Ragamuffin's Path to God*. San Francisco: HarperSanFrancisco, 2000.

Miller, J. R. *The Master's Blesseds: A Devotional Study of the Beatitudes*. New York: Fleming H. Revell Company, 1898.

Ogilvie, Lloyd John. *God's Best for My Life*. Eugene, Ore.: Harvest House Publishers, 1981.

Packer, J. I. *A Quest for Godliness: The Puritan Vision of the Christian Life*. Wheaton, Ill.: Crossway Books, 1990.

Phillips, J. B. *Good News*. London: Geoffrey Bles, 1964.

Smith, Hannah Whitall. *God Is Enough*. Edited by Melvin E. Dieter and Hallie A. Dieter. Grand Rapids, Mich.: Francis Asbury Press, 1986.

Sockman, Ralph W. *The Higher Happiness*. New York: Abingdon-Cokesbury Press, 1950.

Stafford, Tim. "The Church's Walking Wounded: How Should We Respond in a Psychological Age?" *Christianity Today* (March 2003): 64–69.

Volf, Miroslav. *Exclusion and Embrace: A Theological Exploration of Identity, Otherness, and Reconciliation*. Nashville, Tenn.: Abingdon Press, 1996.

Wall, James M. "The Future of a Vision: Religious Journalism in a Post–9/11 World." *Zion's Herald* 176, no. 6, 5–6.

Water, Mark. *A Year with the Saints*. Liguori, Mo.: Liguori Publications, 1997.

Wesley, John. "An Earnest Appeal to Men of Reason and Religion." In *The Works of John Wesley*. Vol. 11, *The Appeals to Men of Reason and Religion and Certain Related Open Letters*. Edited by Gerald R. Cragg. Nashville, Tenn.: Abingdon Press, 1989.

———. "Sermon 12: The Witness of Our Own Spirit." *The Works of John Wesley*. Vol. 1, *Sermons*. Edited by Albert C. Outler. Nashville, Tenn.: Abingdon Press, 1984.

———. "Thoughts upon Methodism." *The Works of John Wesley*. Vol. 9. Nashville, Tenn.: Abingdon Press, 1989.

———. *The Works of John Wesley*. Vol. 18, *Journal and Diaries I: 1735–38*. Edited by W. Reginald Ward and Richard P. Heitzenrater. Nashville, Tenn.: Abingdon Press, 1988.

Wilder, Amos N. *Eschatology and Ethics in the Teaching of Jesus*. Rev. ed. New York: Harper & Brothers, 1950.

A Year with the Saints, Translated by a member of the Order of Mercy (Mt. Joseph's Seminary, Hartford, Conn.). Rockford, Ill.: Tan Books and Publishers, 1988.

AFFIRMATION CARDS

We take every thought captive to obey Christ.

—2 Corinthians 10:5

PRAYER FOR PERSECUTED CHRISTIANS

Pour out your Holy Spirit on

_____ *(insert names of*
persecuted Christians).
May they be for the world the body of Christ, redeemed by his blood.
Make them one with Christ, one with each other, and one in ministry to all
    the world.

—Adapted from "A Service of Word and Table I,"
The Great Thanksgiving, *The United Methodist Hymnal*, No. 10

PETITIONS FROM PSALM 51

Against you, you alone, have I sinned.
Wash me thoroughly from my iniquity, and cleanse me from my sin.
I know my transgressions, and my sin is ever before me.
Create in me a clean heart, O God, and put a new and right spirit within me.
Do not cast me away from your presence, and do not take your holy spirit
    from me.
Restore to me the joy of your salvation.

Who shall ascend the hill of the LORD?
    And who shall stand in his holy place?
Those who have clean hands and pure hearts,
who do not lift up their souls to what is false,
and do not swear deceitfully.

—Psalm 24:3-4

O God, you are my God, I seek you.
    my soul thirsts for you;
my flesh faints for you,
    as in a dry and weary land where there is no water.
So I have looked upon you in the sanctuary,
    beholding your power and glory.
Because your steadfast love is better than life,
    my lips will praise you.
So I will bless you as long as I live;
    I will lift up my hands and call on your name.
My soul is satisfied as with a rich feast,
    and my mouth praises you with joyful lips
when I think of you on my bed, and meditate on you
    in the watches of the night:
for you have been my help
    and in the shadow of your wings I sing for joy.
My soul clings to you;
    your right hand upholds me.

—Psalm 63:1-8

Make me a captive, Lord, and then I shall be free;
Force me to render up my sword, and I shall conqueror be.
I sink in life's alarms when by myself I stand;
Imprison me within thine arms, and strong shall be my hand.

My heart is weak and poor until it master finds;
It has no spring of action sure, it varies with the wind.
It cannot freely move till thou hast wrought its chain;
Enslave it with thy matchless love, and deathless it shall reign.

—Words by George Matheson, 1890 (based on Eph. 3:1)

GRACIOUS GOD,
As your Son wept with Mary and Martha at the tomb of Lazarus, look with
compassion on those who grieve, especially _____,
_____, and _____ (*names*).
Grant them the assurance of your presence now and faith in your eternal goodness, that in them may be fulfilled the promise that those who mourn shall be
comforted; through Jesus Christ our Lord. Amen.

—Laurence Hull Stookey, "For Those Who Mourn," © 1989
The United Methodist Publishing House

LORD, make me an instrument of your peace.
where there is hatred, let me sow love;
where there is injury, pardon;
where there is doubt, faith;
where there is despair, hope;
where there is darkness, light;
where there is sadness, joy.
O Divine Master, grant that I may not so much seek
to be consoled as to console;
to be understood as to understand;
to be loved as to love.
For it is in giving that we receive;
it is in pardoning that we are pardoned;
and it is in dying that we are born to eternal life. Amen.

—Attributed to Saint Francis of Assisi

BLESSED are the poor in spirit, for theirs is the kingdom of heaven.
Blessed are those who mourn, for they will be comforted.
Blessed are the meek, for they will inherit the earth.
Blessed are those who hunger and thirst for righteousness,
    for they will be filled.
Blessed are the merciful, for they will receive mercy.
Blessed are the pure in heart, for they will see God.
Blessed are the peacemakers, for they will be called children of God.
Blessed are those who are persecuted for righteousness' sake, for theirs is the
    kingdom of heaven.

—Matthew 5:3-10

THE LORD is merciful and gracious, slow to anger and abounding in steadfast love.
He will not always accuse, nor will he keep his anger forever. He does not deal with
us according to our sins, nor repay us according to our iniquities. For as the heavens
are high above the earth, so great is his steadfast love toward those who fear him;
as far as the east is from the west, so far he removes our transgressions from us. As
a father has compassion for his children, so the LORD has compassion for those who
fear him. For he knows how we were made; he remembers that we are dust.

—Psalm 103:8-14

ABOUT THE AUTHORS

Maxie Dunnam is chancellor of Asbury Theological Seminary, Wilmore, Kentucky. He served as president of the seminary from 1994 to 2004. Before that, he was senior minister at the six-thousand-member Christ United Methodist Church in Memphis, Tennessee. Maxie was world editor of *The Upper Room* daily devotional guide from 1975 to 1982, and prior to that he served as director of prayer life and fellowship for Upper Room Ministries. Maxie holds a bachelor's degree from the University of Southern Mississippi, a master's in theology from Emory University, and a doctor of divinity from Asbury Theological Seminary. A prolific writer, Maxie has authored more than thirty books, including the widely used *Workbook of Living Prayer*, *This Is Christianity*, *Unless We Pray*, and two volumes in the Communicator's Commentary series. Maxie and his wife, Jerry, have three adult children: Kim, Kerry, and Kevin.

Kimberly Dunnam Reisman, a graduate of Emory University and Yale Divinity School, is United Methodist clergy (North Indiana Conference) and associate pastor of Trinity United Methodist Church in Lafayette, Indiana. A wife and mother of three, Kim is responsible for outreach ministries directed at non-Christian/unchurched persons. She is actively involved in the World Methodist Council, serving on the Executive Committee and working to connect and strengthen ministry to families worldwide. Kim also participates in world evangelism through the Order of the Flame and Faith-Sharing Training Ministries. She is the author of *The Christ-Centered Woman, Knowing God: Making God the Main Thing in My Life*, and *Following at a Distance*. She is coauthor (with Maxie Dunnam) of *The Workbook on the Ten Commandments*, *The Workbook on the Seven Deadly Sins*, and *The Workbook on the Virtues and the Fruit of the Spirit*.

CPSIA information can be obtained
at www.ICGtesting.com
Printed in the USA
LVHW040719250119
605205LV00002B/2/P